50
LITERACY HOURS FOR
LESS ABLE
LEARNERS

- Tricky topics covered
- Shared texts for a lower reading age
- Photocopiable activities

AGES 9-11

Julie Coyne and
Helen Lane

CREDITS

Authors
Helen Lane and
Julie Coyne

Illustrations
Gary Swift

Editor
Victoria Lee

Series Designer
Anna Oliwa

Assistant Editor
Aileen Lalor

Designer
Anna Oliwa

Text © Helen Lane and Julie Coyne
© 2005 Scholastic Ltd

Designed using Adobe InDesign

Published by Scholastic Ltd
Villiers House
Clarendon Avenue
Leamington Spa
Warwickshire CV32 5PR

www.scholastic.co.uk

Printed by Bell & Bain

3456789   5678901234

ACKNOWLEDGEMENTS

The publishers gratefully acknowledge permission to reproduce the following copyright material:
The Authors Licensing and Collecting Society Ltd on behalf of the estate of the late
E V Rieu for 'The Cat's Funeral' by E V Rieu from *The Works*, edited by Paul Cookson © E
V Rieu (2000, Macmillan) and 'The Hippopotamus's Birthday' by E V Rieu from *I like this
poem*, edited by Kaye Webb © E V Rieu (1979, Penguin). **Eugene Blackwood** for 'My Story
Voyage on the Great Titanic' by Eugene Blackwood © 2005, Eugene Blackwood, previously
unpublished. **Laura Cecil Literary Agency** for and behalf of Nicholas Fisk for an extract
from *Time Trap* by Nicholas Fisk © 1976, Nicholas Fisk (1976, Puffin). **Paul Cookson** for
'Where Teachers Keep their Pets' from *Teachers' Pets* by Paul Cookson © 1998, Paul Cookson
(1998, Macmillan). **John Foster** for 'Haikus' from *The Works* edited by Paul Cookson © 2000,
John Foster (2000, Macmillan). **David Higham Associates** for an extract from *The Ghost
of Thomas Kempe* by Penelope Lively © 1973, Penelope Lively (1973, Heinemann). **David
Higham Associates** for an extract from *Boy* by Roald Dahl © 1984, Roald Dahl (1984,
Jonathan Cape Ltd). **David Higham Associates** for an extract from *Kensuke's Kingdom*
by Michael Morpurgo © 1999, Michael Morpurgo (1999, Heinemann). **David Higham
Associates** for 'I Saw a Jolly Hunter' from *Figgie Hobbin* by Charles Causley © 1970, Charles
Causley (1970, Macmillan). **Catherine Marcangeli** Literary Executrix of the late Adrian
Henri, for 'Four Seasons Haiku' by Adrian Henri from *Robocat* by Adrian Henri © 1998, Adrian
Henri (1998, Bloomsbury). **Tony Mitton** for 'Write-a-Rap Rap' from *The Moonlit Streams and
other Poems* by Tony Mitton © 2000, Tony Mitton (2000, Oxford University Press).
The Orion Publishing Group for the blurb from *The Thieves of Ostia* by Caroline Lawrence
© 2001, Caroline Lawrence (2001, Dolphin). **The Penguin Group** for an extract from
The Adventures of Robin Hood by Roger Lancelyn Green © 1956, Roger Lancelyn Green
(1956, Puffin). **The Penguin Group (UK)** for the story synopsis from the front of *The
Hodgeheg* by Dick King-Smith © 1987, The Penguin Group (UK) (1987, Hamish Hamilton).
The Penguin Group (UK) for 'First Day Back' and 'The Question' by Allan Ahlberg from
Heard It in the Playground by Allan Ahlberg © 1989, Allan Ahlberg (1989, Viking). **The
Peters Fraser and Dunlop Group** for the use of 'Haiku' by Roger McGough from *The
Works* edited by Paul Cookson © 2000, Roger McGough (2000, Macmillan) **John Rice** for
'Ettykett' from *Rockets and Quasars* by John Rice © 1984, John Rice (1984, Aten Press).
Usborne Publishing for an extract on Florence Nightingale from *Famous Women* by
Richard Dungworth and Philippa Wingate © 1996, Usborne Publishing Ltd (1996, Usborne
Publishing). **Dave Ward** for 'Maggie and the Dinosaur' by Dave Ward from *The Works* edited
by Paul Cookson © 2000, Dave Ward (2000, Macmillan).

British Library Cataloguing-in-Publication Data
A catalogue record for this book is
available from the British Library.

ISBN 0-439-97179-9
ISBN 978-0439-97179-9

The rights of Helen Lane and Julie Coyne
to be identified as the authors of this work
have been asserted by them in accordance
with the Copyright, Designs and Patents
Act 1988.

Extracts from The National Literacy
Strategy © Crown copyright. Reproduced
under the terms of HMSO Guidance Note
8.

Contents

50 LITERACY HOURS
FOR LESS ABLE LEARNERS AGES 9 TO 11

This series of three books provides a range of activities with the less able learners in any classroom in mind. The activities cover many of the main objectives in the National Literacy Strategy at word, sentence and text level.

Each lesson uses photocopiable games, activities and examples. These are specially designed to help the slower learner understand and develop, and to expand their literacy when reading, writing, speaking and listening. The lesson plans are designed to:
• enable teachers to explain word- and sentence-level work in a simple, step-by-step approach
• guide the writing process by giving the teacher suggestions to model and ideas for sharing and planning in relation to text-level work
• motivate the children with engaging activities and games
• address different learning styles and levels by providing a variety of activities.

About the book
Each book is made up of 50 lesson plans with an accompanying photocopiable activity and, in order to make the book simple to use, the lessons all follow a similar pattern. At the back of the book are photocopiable text extracts that can be used to address the text-level criteria, providing the teacher with good examples from children's literature as and when it is needed.

How to use this book
Each lesson is written to address one or two specific NLS objectives from Years 5 and 6 and these are given at the start of each lesson plan. The grid at the beginning of the book shows tracking back, if the subject area has already been introduced in Years 3 or 4.

These lessons will help you to teach literacy in a creative and inspiring way. The activities are designed for practising and reinforcing learning from the beginning part of the lesson. The independent activities, usually produced as photocopiable sheets, are presented in a variety of formats to try to accommodate a range of learning styles, and the children should be encouraged to work with as little adult support as possible.

The Plenary may be a brief assessment and review, a few more turns of a game or a quick variation on the main activity.

The lessons and accompanying photocopiable activities in the book are written as stand-alone units and can be used by the teacher or teaching assistant at any point in the school year. The activities are designed to fit into the individual teacher's planning for literacy.

Title of lesson	Y6 objective(s)	Y5 objective(s)/tracking back	Y4	Y3
Word sums		**T1: W5** To investigate, collect and classify spelling patterns in pluralisation, construct rules for regular spelling: add *s* to most words; add *es* to *s*, *sh*, *ch*; add *ies* when *y* preceded by consonant; add *s* when *y* preceded by vowel; change *f* to *ves*.	**T1: W7.**	
Plural match		**T1: W5** To investigate, collect and classify spelling patterns in pluralisation, construct rules for regular spellings.	**T1: W7.**	**T2: W11.**
Post boxes		**T2: W5** To investigate words which have common letter strings but different pronunciations.	**T3: W6.**	
Dictionary dash		**T3: W12** To use dictionaries efficiently to explore spellings, meanings, derivations, for example, by using alphabetical order, abbreviations, definitions with understanding.		**T3: W15.** **T2: W19–23.**
Scientific dictionary		**T3: W13** To compile own class/group dictionary using personally written definitions.		**T3: W15.** **T2: W19–23.**
Direct and reported speech		**T1: S5** To understand the difference between direct and reported speech.		**T1: S7-9.** **T3: S4.**
Adding adverbs		**T1: W10** To use adverbs to qualify verbs in writing dialogue, for example, *timidly*, *gruffly*, *excitedly*, using a thesaurus to extend vocabulary.	**T1: S4** **T3: S4.**	**T1: W19.**
Writing speech		**T1: S7** To understand how dialogue is set out.		**T1: S7-9.** **T3: S4.**
Which sense?		**T2: S7** To explore ambiguities that arise from sentence contractions, for example, through signs and headlines.	**T2: S3.**	**T2: S9.**
Connectives	**T1: W6** To investigate meanings and spellings of connectives.	**T3: S7** To use connectives to link clauses within sentences.	**T3: S4.**	
Conditionals	**T2: S5** To use conditionals in the past and future, experimenting with transformations, discussing effects, for example, speculating about possible causes (past) reviewing a range of options and their outcomes (future).			
Proper Names	**T1: W8** To research the origins of proper nouns, for example, place names.			
Active and passive sentences	**T1: S2** To revise earlier work on verbs and understand the terms *active* and *passive*; being able to transform a sentence from active to passive, and vice versa.	**T1: S8** To revise and extend work on verbs.	**T1: S2, S33.**	**T1: S4-5.**
Complex sentences	**T1: S5** To form complex sentences.	**T2: S8** To construct sentences in different ways while retaining meaning. **T2: S9** To secure the use of the comma in embedding clauses within sentences.		
Punctuating complex sentences		**T3: S5** To use punctuation marks accurately in complex sentences.	**T2: S4.**	**T3: S7.**
Proverbs	**T2: W6** To collect and explain the meanings and origins of proverbs.			
Explaining metaphors		**T2: W12** To investigate metaphorical expressions and figures of speech from everyday life.		
Creating metaphors	**T3: W7** To experiment with language, for example, creating new words, similes and metaphors.	**T2: W12** To investigate metaphorical expressions and figures of speech from everyday life.		
Perfect punctuation		**T1: S6** To understand the need for punctuation as an aid to the reader.	**T3: S2.**	**T1: S6.**

NLS OBJECTIVES

Title of lesson	Y6 objective(s)	Y5 objective(s)/tracking back	Y4	Y3
Transforming nouns and verbs.		**T3: W6** To transform words, changing verbs to nouns, for example, *ion, ism, ology* and nouns to verbs, for example, *ise, ify, en.*	T3: W8.	T1: W11. T3: W10.
Words from other languages		**T3: W8** To identify everyday words which have been borrowed from other languages.		
Main and subordinate clauses		**T3: S6** To investigate clauses by identifying the main clause in a long sentence.	T2: S4.	T3: S7.
Adapting writing		**T1: S4** To adapt writing for different readers and purposes by changing vocabulary, tone and sentence structure to suit, for example, simplifying for younger readers.		
Formal language	**T2: S2** To understand features of formal official language.	**T1: S4** To adapt writing for different readers and purposes by changing vocabulary, tone and sentence structures to suit, for example simplifying for younger readers. **T2: S3** To understand how writing can be adapted for different audiences and purposes, for example by changing vocabulary and sentence structures. **T3: S2** To understand how writing can be adapted.		
Book Reviews		**T1: T10** To evaluate a book by referring to details and examples in the text. **T1: T13** To record their ideas, reflections and predictions about a book, for example, through a reading log or journal.		T3: T14.
Myths, legends and fables		**T2: T1** To identify and classify the features of myths, legends and fables, for example, the moral in a fable, fantastical beasts in legends.		T2: T1, 2, & 9.
Point of view		**T2: T8** To distinguish between the author and the narrator, investigating narrative viewpoint and the treatment of different characters.		T1: T3. T2: S10. T3: T3 & 12.
Changing the point of view		**T3: T7** To write from another character's point of view.		
Different genres		**T2: T9** To investigate the features of different fiction genres, for example, science fiction, adventure, discussing the appeal of popular fiction.	T2: T1, 2, 3 & 10.	T1: T1, 2 & 11.
Literal and figurative		**T2: T10** To understand the differences between literal and figurative language.	T2: S1, T2, T4, T5 & 10.	T2: T2 & 11.
Additional dialogue		**T3: T9** To write in the style of the author, for example, writing additional dialogue.		T1; W19, S7, T1, 2 & 10. T3: S4.
Writing a synopsis	**T1: T8** To summarise a passage, chapter or text in a specified number of words. **T3: T10** To write a brief synopsis of a text, for example, for back cover blurb.		T3: T20 &24.	T3: T19 & 26.
Flashback!	**T2: T11** To write own story using, for example, flashbacks or a story within a story to convey the passing of time.		T1: T3. T2: T20.	T3: S5.
The poet's style		**T1: T6** To read a number of poems by significant poets and identify what is distinctive about the style or content of their poems.	T1: T8. T3: T9.	T1: T7.
Writing a rap		**T2: T6** To understand terms which describe different kinds of poems, for example ballad, sonnet, rap, elegy, narrative poem, and to identify typical features. **T2: T12** To use the structures of poems read to write extensions based on these, for example additional verses, or substituting own words and ideas.	T1: T14. T2: T7 & 11.	

Title of lesson	Y6 objective(s)	Y5 objective(s)/tracking back	Y4	Y3
Narrative poems		**T2: T6** To understand terms which describe different kinds of poems, for example, ballad, sonnet, rap, elegy, narrative poem, and to identify typical features. **T2: T12** To use the structures of poems read to write extensions based on these, for example additional verses, or substituting own words and ideas.		T2: T11.
Humorous verse	**T2: T4** To investigate humorous verse: how poets play with meanings; nonsense words and how meaning can be made of them; where the appeal lies.		T1: T14. T2: T11.	T3: T6.
Haiku poetry	**T3: T13** To write a sequence of poems linked by theme or form, for example a haiku calendar.		T1: T14. T3: T5.	
A playscript		**T1: T18** To write own playscript, applying conventions learned from reading; including production notes.	T1: T13.	T1: T15.
Recounting an event		**T1: T21** To identify the features of recounted texts such as sports reports, diaries, police reports. **T1: T24** To write recounts based on subject, topic or personal experiences for (a) a close friend and (b) an unknown reader.		T3: T22.
Clear instructions		**T1: T22 &** To read and evaluate a range of instructional texts in terms of their: purposes; organisation and layout; clarity and usefulness. **T1: T25** To write instructional texts, and test them out, for example instructions for loading computers, design briefs for technology, rules for games.	T1: T22 & 25.	T2: T12, 13, 14, 15 & 16.
Abbreviations		**T1: T23** To discuss the purpose of note-taking and how this influences the nature of notes made. **T1: T27** To use simple abbreviations in note-taking.	T2: T21.	
Taking notes		**T1: T26** To make notes for different purposes. **T1: T27** To use simple abbreviations in note-taking. **T2: T17** to locate information confidently and efficiently through skimming to gain overall sense of text and scanning to locate specific information.	T2: T14, 18 & 21.	T1: T21 & 22. T2: T17. T3: T25.
Non-chronological reports	**T1: T13** To secure understanding of the features of non-chronological reports. **T1: T17** To write non-chronological reports linked to other subjects.	**T2: T22** To plan, compose, edit and refine short non-chronological reports and explanatory texts.	T1: T27. T2: T22.	T1: T23.
Persuasive writing		**T3: T19** To construct an argument in note form or full text to persuade others of a point of view.	T3: T18, 21 & 23.	
Biographies	**T1: T11** To distinguish between biography and autobiography.			
Writing a biography	**T1 T14:** To develop the skills of biographical and autobiographical writing in role, adopting distinctive voices, for example of historical characters.			
A balanced report	**T2: T16** To identify the features of balanced written arguments. **T2: T19** To write a balanced report of a controversial issue.		T3: T16 & 17.	
News articles	**T1: T15** To develop a journalistic style. **T1: T16** To use the styles and conventions of journalism to report on for example real or imagined events.		T1: T20, 21 & 24.	T3: T22.

Word sums

Objective
Y5. T1. W5.
To investigate, collect and classify spelling patterns in pluralisation, construct rules for regular spellings, for example: add *s* to most words; add *es* to most words ending in *s, sh, ch*; change *f* to *ves*; when *y* is preceded by a consonant, change to *ies*; when *y* is preceded by a vowel, add *s*.

Guided work

1. Before the lesson, write a short list on the board of words which come into each of the spelling categories in the objectives, for example: *school, boy, bus, patch, hiss, city, life, scarf*, and so on. Prepare a table with six columns, one for each of the spelling rules including irregular examples. Do not give these columns headings at this stage.

2. Tell the children that they will be investigating plurals, and encourage them to recall what this means by giving examples. Begin with the basic 'adding *s*' for words such as *school, chair* and *dog*. Put these words into the first column. Then ask the children to select singular words from the board and make them plural. Begin sorting the words into the columns on the board, putting like spellings together. As each word changes, discuss the spelling rules that apply. Can the children think of some other words that would fit into the different columns?

3. Begin giving the columns headings – adding '*s*' for the first column. For the second column, ask the children when you should add *es*.

4. Ask the children to explain why *day = days* and *boy = boys*, yet *city = cities* and *worry = worries*. Nouns ending in a consonant and the letter *y* will be changed to add *ies*. For nouns ending in a vowel and the letter *y*, simply add *s*.

5. Ensure all columns have an appropriate heading before the children begin their independent work.

Independent work

● Ask the children to 'calculate' the answer to each word sum on the photocopiable sheet opposite using the rules that were discussed previously. Remind them that they need to apply the rules that have been discussed, rather than just adding on the letter *s*. If necessary, work through the first example on the sheet together. Encourage the children to discuss each word with a partner, identifying which category it would fall into.

Plenary

● Ensure all the children have a whiteboard or paper and pen. Have a selection of irregular words available, for example: *antenna, goose, mouse, tooth* and *child*. Ask the children to write the plural version of the word on to their whiteboard and show you the answer. Add to the table on the board any extra words from the photocopiable activity sheet.

Further support
● Set weekly spellings based on the plural and singular of words.
● Display the singular to plural spelling rules in the classroom.
● Use Look-Say-Cover-Write-Check to practise these words.

Word sums

■ Fill in the missing parts of the calculations.

balloon + s = _____

bus + s = _____

lorry + s = _____

school + s = _____

boy + s = _____

box + s = _____

jelly + s = _____

knife + s = _____

man + s = _____

sisters – s = _____

words – s = _____

foxes – s = _____

cries – s = _____

puppies – s = _____

lunches – s = _____

loaves – s = _____

thieves – s = _____

halves – s = _____

_____ ? + s = houses

_____ ? + s = girls

_____ ? + s = babies

_____ ? + s = watches

_____ ? + s = churches

_____ ? + s = lollies

party + s = _____

self + s = _____

woman + s = _____

kitten + s = _____

■ Now try some of your own.

_____ + s = _____   _____ – s = _____

_____ + s = _____   _____ – s = _____

Plural match

Objective
Y5. T1. W5.
To investigate, collect and classify spelling patterns in pluralisation, construct rules for regular spellings.

Guided work

1. Remind the children of the spelling rules covered previously:

- add *s* to most words
- add *es* to *s, sh, ch*
- add *ies* when *y* preceded by consonant
- add *s* when *y* preceded by vowel
- change *f* to *ves*
- irregular examples.

2. Begin by asking the children to use their whiteboards to show you a word which fits the first spelling rule - adding *s*. Spend ten minutes asking a series of closed questions which all children can respond to using their whiteboards, for example: *What is the plural of church? Which rule does the word 'puppy' fit? How many words can you think of in 30 seconds which fit the 'f' to 'ves' rule?*

3. Organise the children into similar-ability pairs and provide each pair with a set of word cards from the photocopiable sheet opposite. (The task can be made easier by removing the irregular words, or more difficult by adding extra examples.)

4. Tell the children that they will be playing a game of 'Plural snap'. The idea of the game is to spot two cards which have the same plural rule. The first player to spot the rule says, 'Snap!' If they have correctly identified the rule, the player wins the cards. The winner is the player with the most cards when the game finishes.

5. As the children play the game, encourage them to say their plural word as they place their singular word card on the table, for example: as they place *bus* down on the table, they say '*buses*'.

Independent work

- Ask the children to sort their word cards into piles, one for each rule. Let the children transfer these lists into books or spelling logs, writing both the singular and plural version of each word.

Plenary

- Again working in similar-ability pairs, ask the children to take turns to test each other on the spellings which have been covered. The child testing can select words randomly from the word cards. The speller can write responses on their mini-whiteboard or paper. Take feedback on how well the children managed this task.

Further support
- Have the columns already written into books or spelling logs before the lesson.
- Display the list of spelling rules revised at the start of the lesson.

Plural match

school	boy	girl
balloon	brother	sister
bus	church	lunch
fox	brush	dish
box	lorry	baby
city	party	puppy
lolly	jelly	thief
half	knife	calf
wolf	goose	mouse
tooth	die	antenna

Letter-string postboxes

Objective
Y5. T2. W5.
To investigate words which have common letter strings but different pronunciations.

Guided work

1. Before the lesson, prepare six large envelopes, one for each common letter string (*ight*, *ear*, *oo*, *ough*, *ie*, *our*). Enlarge the photocopiable sheet to make a set of 'teacher' word cards. Use the blank cards to add your own words.

2. Begin by telling the children that they will be sorting words into categories depending upon their spelling. Select one of the word cards to begin with, for example, *pear*. Say the word clearly to the children before you reveal the spelling. Can the children hear the common letter string? Which of the envelopes should this card be posted into?

3. Continue to select word cards, clearly saying the word to the children and asking who can hear which envelope the card should be posted into.

Independent work

● Organise the children into pairs. Provide each pair with a set of word cards and the means to sort them - either a set of envelopes or sorting rings. Ask the children to take it in turns to pick up a card and say the word clearly to their partner. Their partner will need to listen very carefully and decide which envelope or ring the word should be placed into. Encourage the children to keep taking turns at selecting a card until all of the cards are sorted. When all the words are sorted, ask the children to look separately at each common letter string and to see what they notice about how the words are pronounced. Encourage the children to investigate this as independently as they can by giving them hints, for example: *Is the **ear** in p**ear** pronounced the same way as the **ear** in g**ear**? What do you notice about the different ways **ight** can be pronounced?*

Further support
● Provide a sorting table for the children to use as a frame when sorting the word cards.
● Use a set of questions to prompt the investigation at the end of the independent work. Different groups could be given different questions depending upon ability.

Plenary

● Ask the children what they noticed as they were sorting the word cards (the different letter strings were pronounced in different ways depending upon the word). In which particular words did the children notice this? Ask for children to give two words which have the same letter string but different pronunciation and encourage a response from each pair in the room. Use the sorted lists to demonstrate to the children that the pronunciation can depend upon the following sounds, for example: an *e* before *igh* usually means that it has a long *ay* sound, as in *weight*.

● Also point out that pronunciation can be altered by regional dialect. The children may have experiences they can share on this.

Letter-string postboxes

right	pear	book	lie	colour	cough
light	bear	food	pie	favour	dough
night	search	cook	niece	neighbour	enough
eight	wear	good	piece	pour	plough
weight	year	hook	tried	your	thought
tight	learn	mood	field	hour	drought
height	ear	pool	shield	flour	though
clear	root	thieves	rumour	earth	boot
tie	honour	tear	foot	fried	armour

Dictionary dash

Objective
Y5. T3. W12.
To use dictionaries efficiently to explore spellings, meanings, derivations, for example, by using alphabetical order, abbreviations, definitions with understanding.

Guided work

1. Before the lesson begins, ensure there are enough dictionaries and photocopiable sheets for one each. Also take the time to check that the words listed on the sheet are in the dictionaries you have in class.

2. Begin the lesson by recapping the purposes of a dictionary. Remind the children that, as well as providing spellings and definitions, the dictionaries also classify words and can assist with pronunciation. Discuss the alphabetical layout of the dictionary.

3. Give the children a word relevant to current science work to look up, for example, *gravity*. Encourage the children to work silently and put a hand up when their finger is on the word *gravity*.

4. Ask one of the children to read out their definition. If there are several different dictionaries in the room, ask the children to give definitions from the different dictionaries.

5. Invite the children who found the word very quickly to explain their method. Discuss the letter '*g*' as the seventh letter of the alphabet which is towards the beginning of the dictionary and so on.

6. Select another three or four relevant words and ask the children to look them up as quickly as they can.

7. Ask the children to confirm the spellings of the words.

Independent work

● Place one copy of the photocopiable sheet face down on the table in front of each child and make sure the children are prepared. Explain that there are ten words on the sheet and the children must look them all up as quickly as they can. For each word, they need to write the definition on to the sheet. Negotiate a reward for the quickest workers in the dictionary dash - stickers, team points and so on. Give the children an *on your marks, get set, GO!* Throughout the session give the children regular time prompts to keep them focused.

Further support
● Provide easier dictionaries for children who will struggle with this activity.
● Keep the vocabulary displayed in the classroom and encourage the children to use it on a daily basis.

Plenary

● Ask the children to share their definitions for each of the words. Encourage correct pronunciation of important vocabulary.
● To end the lesson, ask the children to put the vocabulary into context by putting it into a sentence. Reward longer, complex sentences that really explain the word, for example: *I initiated a game of football on the playground today and we all had fun!*
● Let children say interesting words they may have recently learned. Other children can then look them up.

Dictionary dash

■ Look up these new words in a dictionary. Write out the definitions.

audacious _____

_____

cherish _____

_____

elude _____

_____

initiate _____

_____

liberate _____

_____

putrid _____

_____

reprimand _____

_____

sublime _____

_____

treacherous _____

_____

versatile _____

_____

50 LITERACY HOURS FOR LESS ABLE
LEARNERS: Ages 9-11

Scientific dictionary

Objective
Y5. T3. W13.
To compile own class/
group dictionary using
personally written
definitions.

Guided work

1. This activity is intended to generate a full scientific dictionary for your class. First, decide how many pages your class dictionary will have, and make enough copies of the photocopiable sheet opposite. Letters could be grouped together, especially, for example, x, y and z, and the dictionary can be tailored to the topics you are studying.

2. Begin the lesson by recapping previous dictionary work (see 'Dictionary dash' on page 14). Ask the children what dictionaries are useful for, how they are used, and how they are set out.

3. Show the children a few examples of subject-specific dictionaries, then tell the children that they will be compiling a dictionary of scientific words and phrases for the class. Each pair will be working on one, two or three letters of the alphabet and compiling a page of the scientific dictionary.

4. In shared writing, compile the first page together. Ask the children to brainstorm scientific words or phrases beginning with the letter.

5. When these words are listed on the board, ask the children to put them into alphabetical order. Discuss using the second and third letter of the word.

6. Model how to write definitions. Try to encourage the children not just to put the word into a sentence but to add detail, for example:

> **Amphibian:** an animal that lives in water and on land; when young has gills but later develops lungs and breathes air.

7. Ask one or two children to spot-check a couple of the definitions in a published dictionary.

Independent work

● Ensure the children work in pairs to think initially of the four or five words or phrases that will be on their page. They can use scrap paper to work on, listing these in alphabetical order and drafting definitions. Then ask the children to write up their words and definitions on a copy of the photocopiable sheet opposite. Encourage the children to work collaboratively by asking both children to write out two definitions.

Plenary

● Take feedback on the definitions, one from each page perhaps, and collect the pages in alphabetical order. Encourage the children to read and check their definitions before handing their work in.

Further support
● Provide a list of scientific words for children who will struggle to think of their own.
● Children who really struggle could simply be asked to match the definition to the word as an activity.
● The collated dictionary could then be kept available for children to use in their science work.

Scientific dictionary

Word: _____

Definition: _____

_____

_____

Word: _____

Definition: _____

_____

_____

Word: _____

Definition: _____

_____

_____

Word: _____

Definition: _____

_____

_____

Direct and reported speech

Guided work

1. Before the lesson, write up a selection of examples of direct and reported speech. Use the names of the children in your class to add interest, for example: *Tom asked Aaron if he wanted to play football at playtime. 'Do you want some crisps?' Bhavna asked Sarah.*

2. Start the lesson by explaining to the children that they will be looking at the differences between direct and reported speech. Ask for suggestions on what these terms mean.

3. Explain that you have a selection of examples on the board and ask the children to discuss with a partner which are examples of direct speech and which are reported.

4. After taking feedback from the children, reiterate that for direct speech, the words actually spoken are recorded, and in text this is indicated by the use of speech marks. For reported (indirect) speech, the writer uses the third person to *explain* what has been said, without necessarily using the words spoken. Note that in reported speech there will not be speech marks. Spend a few minutes taking each example from the board and classifying it as either direct or reported speech.

5. Quickly read the extract on photocopiable page 109 and confirm with the children whether it includes direct or reported speech. How do they know?

Independent work

● Give the children a copy of the photocopiable sheet opposite. Explain that in the first part, they will be turning direct speech into reported speech, and in the second part, they will be doing the opposite. Remind the children of the need to punctuate direct speech accurately by having the correct punctuation marks both inside and outside of the speech marks.

Plenary

● To end the session, ask the children to work in pairs on the examples of direct and reported speech on the board from the beginning of the lesson. Ask for pairs to come to the front and alter the direct speech into reported speech and vice versa.

50 LITERACY HOURS FOR LESS ABLE
LEARNERS: Ages 9-11

Direct and reported speech

◀ Turn these sentences of direct speech into reported speech.

1. 'Let's play basketball,' Adam suggested.

2. 'Can you pass me the pencil?' Sarah asked Joanne.

3. 'Be quiet!' snapped Ruth.

4. 'I'm not your friend any more,' Hassan told Peter.

5. 'Make sure you finish your work,' Mr Smith told the class.

◀ Turn these sentences of reported speech into direct speech.

1. Stuart denied punching Philip on the nose.

2. Jessica asked Stacy for help with her spellings.

3. Jeremiah told Anne that Mr Brown wanted to see her.

4. Ryan asked Daniel to take the football outside.

5. Helen invited Gordon round to her house for tea.

◀ Now try one of your own

Reported speech:

Direct speech:

Adding adverbs

Objective
Y5. T1. W10.
To use adverbs to qualify verbs in writing dialogue, for example, *timidly*, *gruffly*, *excitedly*, using a thesaurus to extend vocabulary.

Guided work

1. Begin the lesson by revising work on direct speech (see 'Direct and reported speech' on page 18). Remind the children that we do not always want to use the word *said* when writing dialogue, as it can become repetitive and boring. Ask the children to begin by contributing to a list of synonyms for *said*. These can be presented as a mind map or brainstorm on the board.

2. Explain that these words are a good start, but that the children can also qualify speech by using an adverb along with the verb to make their work even more interesting and descriptive.

3. Read photocopiable page 109 and highlight the uses of *said* and its various synonyms. Then ask the children to suggest adverbs that could be included, such as: *he said cheerily; shouted the stranger angrily; answered Robin firmly.*

4. Remind the children that the adverb describes the verb and so, in the case of speech, an adverb is added outside the speech marks. Give the children the example, *'Yes please,' said Peter enthusiastically.* Ask them to pretend to be Peter and to say, *'Yes please'*, showing enthusiasm dramatically.

5. Change the adverb to contrast with the first (*quietly, solemnly, meekly* and so on). How would the children now interpret the character of Peter? The children will see how the addition of the adverb, as well as the verb, offers the writer the chance to describe further how the words are spoken.

6. Use other sentences on the board and ask the children to interpret these in a similar way. The children should notice the fact that many adverbs end in the suffix *ly*. Some adverbs do not end in this suffix, such as adverbs that answer when or where (for example, *today*).

Independent work

● Ask the children to complete the speech sentences on the photocopiable sheet opposite by adding the best adverb they can find. Demonstrate how they can use a thesaurus to find more interesting vocabulary, for example: by looking up *quickly*, they would come up with *immediately*. Insist on a ban on boring words!

Plenary

● Ask the children to read out the spoken aspect of their sentences as a performance to the group. Can the other children suggest from the expression what the adverb might be? Begin to make a list of good adverbs on the board.

Further support
● The activity could be completed collaboratively enabling less able pupils to discuss their work. For homework ask the children to produce an adverb alphabet - one adverb for each letter of the alphabet.
● Display a class adverb alphabet of great adverbs and encourage the children to use these each time they write.

Adding adverbs

I can use adverbs to qualify speech.

■ Complete each of these sentences with an adverb to describe how the words are spoken. Remember, boring adverbs are banned; use a thesaurus!

1. 'Why do I have to tidy my room?' said Ruth _____

2. Jim asked _____ 'Nan, can I have sweets from the shop?'

3. 'I'm fed up', Sarah said _____

4. 'Have you taken my crisps?' Paul said _____

5. 'No I haven't!' said Nathan _____

6. Sue whispered _____ 'Did anyone hear anything?'

7. 'I love my music!' said Dean _____

8. 'Can you hear the thunder?' Joshua asked _____

9. 'I'm not your friend any more!' said Sinead _____

10. _____ Julie said 'What was that noise?'

■ For each of these boring adverbs find another more interesting adverb:

quietly _____   **slowly** _____

happily _____   **sadly** _____

quickly _____   **bravely** _____

50 LITERACY HOURS FOR LESS ABLE
LEARNERS: Ages 9–11

Writing speech

Objective
Y5. T1. S7.
To understand how
dialogue is set out.

Guided work

1. Before the lesson, prepare one copy per child of the comic strip on the photocopiable sheet opposite, and choose a short extract of dialogue from the texts at the back of this book.

2. Discuss what the children already know about speech. Explain to the children that they will be writing speech, trying to follow all of the rules and conventions.

3. Show the children the dialogue extract. Ask the children to discuss in pairs what three rules they could apply to the dialogue example. Give the children two minutes of talking time before you take feedback.

4. As the children feed back, write the rules up. Make sure the children have the following rules.

- Speech marks are used around what is spoken.
- Punctuation is needed inside and outside the speech marks.
- A new line is needed for a new speaker.

5. Using the following examples, show the children that the same direct speech can be written differently, but that the same punctuation rules apply each time.

- 'If you hurry,' said the teacher, 'we will be able to finish our work before playtime.'
- The teacher said, 'If you hurry, we will be able to finish our work before playtime.'
- 'If you hurry, we will be able to finish our work before playtime,' said the teacher.

Independent work

- Ask volunteers to talk through the cartoon, one frame at a time. Initially, the children can simply describe what they see, but then these thoughts need to be formalised into the narrative style. Begin the activity as a whole class, scribing the dialogue for the first frame.
- The children then continue the activity independently, using the speech bubbles as the basis for the dialogue they will write.

Plenary

- Ask the children to work in pairs to edit and mark their speech. Refer them to the list of rules that you wrote together and ask them to check that their partner has followed these rules.

Further support
- Children who find independent writing more difficult could be given a writing frame to follow that already has the verbs and characters written in. The children would then simply be concentrating on the direct speech and its punctuation.

Writing speech

■ Write the speech taking place in the cartoon.

Sentences make sense

Guided work

1. Explain to the children that sometimes when sentences are shortened, their meaning can become unclear. Give the children the example of several friends meeting for dinner. One dinner guest says to the others: 'We are waiting for Richard to eat.' Discuss why the meaning of the sentence may be unclear. Ask the children to explain both meanings of the sentence.

2. Explain to the children that newspaper and magazine headlines are usually made up of sentence contractions. Very often they do not make complete sense on their own and the rest of the report is needed to clarify the full meaning.

Independent work

● Put the children into groups of three or four, and provide each with one of the headlines from the photocopiable sheet opposite. Explain that each group will perform two sketches, one for each of the possible meanings of the sentence. Use one of the headlines as an example to discuss and explain. This could then be given to a group that would benefit from extra support.

● Tell the children that one of their two sketches could be funny as it will show the nonsensical aspect of the sentence. Set clear guidelines about the use of props, noise levels and physical contact. Give the groups plenty of room to act out their pieces and a time limit of about 20 minutes to prepare.

Plenary

● Ask the groups to sit round together as an audience. Watch each group in turn perform their two different sketches. Take time after each group to discuss the ambiguities that arose in their sentence. Ask the children to tell you how they knew which was the real meaning of each sentence.

Further support
● Some children will find speaking and performing to a group very difficult and will need plenty of encouragement to build their self-confidence. The more frequently the children are given opportunities to do this, the easier it will become.
● Children who struggle with the understanding of contracted sentences could perform a headline search in a daily newspaper, giving them the opportunity to read the opening paragraphs of articles which further explain the headline.

50 LITERACY HOURS FOR LESS ABLE
LEARNERS: Ages 9–11

Which sense?

Police shoot youth with knife.

Fire brigade rescue woman with cat.

Paramedics save man with broken leg.

Neighbours row over eight-metre hedge.

Drunken man attacks woman with child.

Youths torment pensioner with garden gnomes.

Stuntman smashes bike with stabilisers.

Footballer scores past goalkeeper with glasses.

Pop star attacks journalist with camera.

Connectives

Guided work

1. Remind the children that connectives are the words and phrases which link or bind an overall text together.

2. Write three short sentences on the board: *It was snowing. Sam went to the shops. He got lost.* Explain that these three short sentences can all be joined together to form a longer, more complex sentence: *It was snowing and Sam went to the shops and got lost.* Here the connective is simple and the three original sentences simply become clauses within a complex sentence.

3. Ask the children how else these sentences could be connected together. The children might give the following examples.

- Although it was snowing, Sam went to the shops. He got lost.
- Sam walked to the shops in the snow and got lost.
- Sam got lost as he walked to the shops in the snow.
- Despite the snow, Sam walked to the shops but got lost on the way.

4. For each example, make it clear what the connecting word or phrase is, and begin making a connectives list for the children. Some of the most common connectives are: *and, but, or, finally, nevertheless, before, although, despite* and *meanwhile*.

5. Point out that the connective does not necessarily occur in the middle of the sentence.

Independent work

- Give all of the children a copy of the photocopiable sheet opposite. Explain that each sentence pair needs to be joined with a connecting word or phrase.

Plenary

- Ask the children to read out their new connected sentences. Look for examples where the choice of connective might affect the meaning of the sentence, for example: *John was angry with Michael <u>so</u> he punched him on the nose. John was angry with Michael <u>because</u> he punched him on the nose.*

Further support
- Ask the children to perform a connective search in their reading books.
- Keep a class connectives list on display and encourage the children to use a connective each time they write.

Connectives

◼ Use connectives to link the clauses within these sentences.

1. The dog barked. Jane ran down the road.

2. Mum changed channel. The TV programme was boring.

3. I was excited. The party would start in less than an hour.

4. Mum was telling me off. My bedroom was a mess.

5. The driver saw the accident. He slowed down.

6. John was angry with Michael. He punched him on the nose.

7. Mum would not take me to the shops. She was in a bad mood.

8. We found the cinema easily. It was marked on the map.

9. Ruth was late for work. The bus was delayed.

10. David was late for school. He said he would be early.

◼ Now try writing some sentences of your own with the following connectives:

| finally | nevertheless | although | until | consequently |

More connectives

Objective
Y6. T1. W6.
To investigate meanings and spellings of connectives.

Guided work

1. Ensure that each table has access to dictionaries before the start of the lesson.

2. Start by telling the children that they will be investigating new connectives. Ask the children to list some simple connectives that they already know, for example: *and, but, so* and *finally*. Explain that there are a wide variety of other connectives available to them. They are going to investigate these other connectives and then begin to use them in their writing.

Independent work

● Put the children into pairs and look at the list of seven connectives in the first activity on the photocopiable sheet opposite. Explain to the children that they must write a definition for each of the connectives in the space provided. They may use a dictionary if they like, but if they feel they know what the word means, they should write a definition of their own. Encourage the children to discuss each definition with their partner before they write anything down. Ensure the definitions explain the purpose of the connective, for example: *in addition, opposition, explaining, listing, indicating time, indicating result* and so on.

● Once all of the children are familiar with the meanings of the connectives, they can begin to use them in their writing. Ask the children to look at the second activity on the photocopiable sheet. For each connective, they must write one or two sentences which will demonstrate their understanding of the word. An example would be: *I had to tidy my room before I was allowed to have my pocket money.* Encourage the children to work as independently as they can.

Plenary

● Ask the children to read out their sentences. Look for examples where connectives are used in different places in the sentence - they may open the sentence or be in the middle.

Further support
● Some children will struggle with ideas for sentences. Offer those children more support by giving them sentence starters, for example: *Sarah was tired from swimming, Jon ran to school, The dog barked at the postman, My brother fell off his bike* and so on. The children can then add to these using the connectives from the list.

More connectives

■ Find out and write down the meanings of these connectives

1. before _____

_____

2. moreover _____

_____

3. nevertheless _____

_____

4. consequently _____

_____

5. in due course _____

_____

6. simultaneously _____

7. furthermore _____

_____

■ Now use the connectives in sentences.

1. before _____

2. moreover _____

3. nevertheless _____

4. consequently _____

5. in due course _____

6. simultaneously _____

7. furthermore _____

50 LITERACY HOURS FOR LESS ABLE
LEARNERS: Ages 9-11

Conditionals

Objective
Y6. T2. S5.
To explore use of conditionals in past and future, experimenting with transformations, discussing effects, for example, speculating about possible causes (past) reviewing a range of options and their outcomes (future).

Guided work

1. Explain to the children that a conditional verb tells us what might happen, because the action depends upon something or somebody else. *Should, would* and *could* tell us that verbs are conditional.

2. Ask the children to come up with sentences using the three words, for example: *We could go to the cinema if you finish your homework.*

3. Explain to the children that the conjunction *if* is often used in the conditional. Ask the children to complete a sentence, such as: *If I won millions on the lottery then…* Give each child in the group a chance to respond and reward any particularly inventive or humorous sentences.

4. Complete the first two sentences on the photocopiable sheet opposite as a group, so that the process is modelled to the children. Explain that the sentences are in pairs, as the verb tense is important in understanding the sentence. For example, *If I water the garden the flowers will grow. If I had watered the garden the flowers would not have died.*

Independent work

● Ask the children to finish off each sentence on the photocopiable sheet opposite in the space provided. Encourage them to think of their own endings for the sentences in the first section and to think about everyday speech and conversations between themselves and their families for the second part of the activity. Give the children about 20 minutes to complete the work.

Plenary

● Classify the sentences that the children have written into past, present and future speculations and outcomes. As the children share their sentences, ask them to classify each section, for example: *If I work hard at school* (present) *then I will go to university* (future).

● Finally, ask the children to share their examples of conditionals from everyday life. Encourage each child to contribute to a discussion on this. Do any of the children have a similar conditional word with a different outcome? *If you wash up, you can have pocket money. If you wash up, we can go shopping.*

Further support
● Allow children who might struggle to work with a more able partner. The sheet could be enlarged to A3 for paired work.
● Ask the children to listen out for conditionals at home, for example: *if you tidy your bedroom you can go out to play* and so on.

Conditionals

◼ Finish these conditional sentences in the past and future tenses.

1a. If I water the garden _____

1b. If I had watered the garden _____

2a. If I won money _____

2b. If I had won money _____

3a. If I take the dog for a walk _____

3b. If I had taken the dog for a walk _____

4a. If I work hard at school _____

4b. If I had worked hard at school _____

5a. If my sister upsets me again _____

5b. If my sister had upset me again _____

◼ Now try to think of examples of conditionals that you have heard in everyday life.
◼ Write some sentences.

_____

_____

_____

_____

_____

Proper names

Objective
Y6. T1. W8.
To research the origins of proper names, for example, place names.

Guided work

1. Before the lesson, take the time to fully prepare resources relevant to your area of the country. This means that the children will see the value and significance of their research. Have a map of your region; you can download these from many websites, for example, www.streetmap.co.uk. Also select a list of relevant place names from www.domesdaybook.co.uk, which is a site that lists the Roman, Celtic, Saxon and Viking origins of place names.

2. Ask the children to give you some examples of proper names. Hopefully you should have a few suggestions of towns, cities, counties or countries.

3. Ensure each child can see a list of place name origins and a relevant map. Explain to the children that they will be researching the origins of local place names, trying to discover the meanings behind the names. Give the children the example of Birmingham. This is an Anglo-Saxon name made from three parts: *ing* means *people of that place, ham* means *village* so *Birm-ing-ham* means *the village of the people of Birm.*

4. Give the children other examples of parts of names which help explain the origin, for example: *ford is a place to cross a river* and *minster is a place where there was a church.*

5. Take the children through some examples from their own locality.

Further support
● Children who find this activity difficult could initially find place names that they felt had a historical origin, before having further support to then find the meaning.
● If your locality is lacking in historical place names, the children could research their own first name on www.behindthename.com, which has a variety of names from different countries. Remind the children that their names, like the names of places, are also proper names.

Independent work

● Ask the children to work in pairs. Instruct them to find place names on the map and try to link them back to their Roman, Saxon, Celtic or Viking origins. The children should fill in the details that they find on the photocopiable sheet opposite. If necessary, talk the children through one or two examples until they are comfortable with the task.

Plenary

● Ask the children to feed back to the group about places local to them. Can the children apply the name origins to any other well-known cities, such as Manchester, Edinburgh, Bath and so on?

Proper names

■ Research the origins of proper names.

Place name	Roman/Saxon/Celtic/ Viking	Meaning

50 LITERACY HOURS FOR LESS ABLE
LEARNERS: Ages 9-11

Active and passive

Objective
Y6. T1. S2.

To revise earlier work on verbs and to understand the terms *active* and *passive*; being able to transform a sentence from active to passive, and vice versa.

Guided work

1. Have a variety of objects available to the children.

2. Introduce or remind the children of the terms *active* and *passive*. Explain that a verb is active when the subject of the verb is performing the action, for example: *Steven broke the television.* Steven is the subject and he is performing the action. The opposite of this is the passive voice. A verb is passive when the action is being performed on the subject by someone else, for example: *The television was broken by Steven.* The television is now the subject of the sentence and the verb applies to it. It may help at this stage to look up the terms *active* and *passive* in a dictionary, or to try and place them into a more realistic context.

3. Provide the children with several more active and passive sentences, perhaps using the following examples.

John parked the car.	The car was parked by John.
Sue wrote the letter.	The letter was written by Sue.
The cat killed the bird.	The bird was killed by the cat.

Independent work

● When you feel the children have been through enough examples, ask them to work in similar-ability pairs. Explain that they are to take it in turns to perform an action upon an object. Their partner must then say the sentence in the passive form. For example, if Peter moves the chair, his partner must say: *The chair was moved by Peter.* Give the children five minutes to perform as many actions as possible.
● Explain to the children that they must now try to use their knowledge to alter sentences. Give each child a copy of the photocopiable sheet opposite. Read the first question to the children and model answering it. Encourage them to complete the remaining sentences independently.

Further support

● When the children are performing actions in their paired work, take photographs of the activity. These could then be used to prompt further discussion or to review the topic.
● Take the time to look for examples of passive sentences used naturally in children's writing. Wherever possible, point these sentences out to the class.

Plenary

● Take brief feedback on the sentences the children have written.
● Ask the children to search through reading or library books for examples of passive sentences. Act as a scribe and write these sentences up as the children find them. Discuss any ambiguities as they arise.
● Help the children to appreciate that, by using passive sentences in their writing, they add variety to their sentence structure and improve the overall quality of their written work.

Active and passive

◀ Turn these sentences from active to passive.

1. The football smashed Mrs Johnson's window.

_____

2. My football team won the league.

_____

3. The dog bit my friend Joseph.

_____

4. Lightning struck the washing line.

_____

5. The children stroked the newborn kittens.

_____

◀ Turn these sentences from passive to active.

1. Our house was painted by Mr Allen.

_____

2. The vase was dropped by my brother.

_____

3. The comedian was cheered by the audience.

_____

4. The cat was run over by the car.

_____

5. The drinks were spilled all over the table by the clumsy waiter.

_____

50 LITERACY HOURS FOR LESS ABLE LEARNERS: Ages 9-11

Complex sentences

Objective
Y6. T1. S5.
To form complex
sentences.

Guided work

1. Prepare enough simple sentence cards for one set between two. Have an enlarged set made and laminated for group demonstration. The children will also need large sheets of paper, one between two, and glue sticks (or they could use ICT).

2. Begin the lesson by telling the children that they will be learning how to improve the quality of their sentences. Explain that a simple sentence is usually quite short and makes sense on its own. Give the children several examples of simple sentences, and ask them to come up with a few of their own, for example: *Caroline walked the dog.*

3. Demonstrate that these simple sentences can be made into complex sentences by adding another clause: *Even though it was pouring with rain, Caroline walked the dog.* An alternative might be: *Caroline walked the dog in the pouring rain.*

4. Ask a volunteer to select one of your simple sentence cards. Share this card with the children. Ask them to talk with a partner and think of another clause that could be added to the sentence to make it complex. Write the suggestions you are given up on the board; there should be plenty of ideas.

Independent work

● Explain to the children that they have 15 simple sentence cards and that they are to work in pairs to extend these simple sentences into better-quality, complex sentences. Tell the children to pick the sentence they would like to start with and devise between the two of them the complex sentence. The children then need to write their new sentence out on their paper, gluing the simple sentence in at the appropriate point. The location of the original simple sentence within the complex sentence is not important. The children may choose to have: *Squealing with delight, <u>the girls skipped down the road,</u>* or: <u>*The girls skipped down the road*</u> *trying not to be late for their tea.*

Plenary

● Ask each pair to present their final sheet of complex sentences to the class and read out their best example.
● These sheets could be displayed around the room or on the board, so that all of the children can share in the sentences.

Further support
● Children who lack their own ideas could add pre-written clauses to the simple sentence cards given on the photocopiable sheet. The activity would then be matching the correct main clause to its subordinate clause to make the complex sentence make sense.

Complex sentences

the girls skipped down the road

the train screeched into the station

the car raced through the country lanes

the postman delivered the package to Susan

the timer on the oven rang

the bicycle was to be his birthday present

the wind whistled through the chimney

Sam wanted to go to the shops

Sarah was crying

Richard hated history lessons

Kathryn wanted to go home

Daniel always made his friends laugh

Laura sulked all afternoon

Elliott was eaten by a monster

Monica had eaten all of the chocolate cake

Punctuating complex sentences

Objective
Y5. T3. S4.
To use punctuation marks accurately in complex sentences.

Guided work

1. Prepare on the board a range of simple sentences which have no punctuation at all.

2. Ask the children to edit the simple sentences, adding all necessary punctuation.

3. Discuss the punctuation added: capital letters, exclamation marks, question marks and full stops.

4. Ask the children which punctuation marks, if any, were perhaps not essential in these simple sentences. Discuss the purpose of commas (a short break marking the relationship between parts of the sentence, or perhaps they have been used as parentheses, identifying subordinate clauses). Begin with an easy example, such as: *The film was really funny so I enjoyed it.* Can the children hear where the comma should be placed?

5. Provide the children with several more examples on the board for them to punctuate. Use the children's names and circumstances to make the sentences more interesting.

Independent work

● Give each of the children a copy of the photocopiable sheet opposite. Explain that the children have ten complex sentences that have no punctuation. Ask the children to add the correct punctuation.
● Encourage the children to read the sentences aloud, so that they can listen out for the punctuation as they read.

Plenary

● Ask the children to mark their own sentences, taking one different aspect of punctuation at a time.
● The children can feed back on how many of the fifteen capital letters they found and so on. This will provide a thorough assessment of which children are forgetting capital letters, full stops and commas.

Further support
● Children who are finding it difficult to add commas should first focus on capitalisation and full stops and more 'obvious' punctuation. Then these children can work in groups to decide where the comma should be placed in each sentence.

Punctuating complex sentences

Add appropriate punctuation to these complex sentences.

1. i cannot play outside today because i feel ill

2. sam wanted to sing in the school choir as her voice was amazing

3. when the sales have started he will go to the shops

4. i do not like sarah so i will not share my sweets with her

5. my cousin was very clever but he did not pass his exams

6. my mum did not buy the computer even though it was half price

7. the shop did not make enough money so they sold it

8. the driver shouted at the girl who had run out into the road without looking

9. diwali the hindu celebration is a festival of lights

10. roald dahl the famous author wrote many children books

50 LITERACY HOURS FOR LESS ABLE
LEARNERS: Ages 9-11

Proverbs

Objective
Y6. T2. W6.
To collect and explain the meanings and origins of proverbs.

Guided work

1. Tell the children that they are going to be explaining the meanings of proverbs.

2. Explain that proverbs do not usually mean exactly what they say, but they are nuggets of wisdom that should be interpreted to teach us something more general. Give the children the example, *You can't have your cake and eat it*, and ask if they know what it means. Explain that in a wider context, the proverb means that you cannot always have everything that you might want in life. Give the children practical examples where this proverb may be heard or applied.

3. Ask the children to think of proverbs they have heard and how they might be used. They may suggest some of the following examples:

When the cat's away, the mice will play. (Children misbehaving because their mother has left them alone.)
Better late than never. (A child is late for school, which is better than not turning up at all.)
Many hands make light work. (If all the children help to tidy their classroom, then each of them only has a small amount of work.)
Too many cooks spoil the broth. (Many children help to make a leaving card for a teacher. The design becomes ruined, because all of the children want to stick things on.)
Never judge a book by its cover. (A new child arrives in school looking different from the other children. The children should take the time to get to know the new child before they judge.)
A stitch in time saves nine. (A car starts rattling and the owner gets it serviced, rather than letting the problem get worse.)

Independent work

● Explain to the children that they need to take one proverb on the photocopiable sheet opposite at a time (the order does not matter) and try to write the meaning of the proverb underneath.
● Allow the children to discuss the meaning of the proverbs in groups, as some children will be more familiar with them than others.

Plenary

● Ask the children to explain each of the six proverbs in turn. Make sure that each of the explanations applies the proverb generally.
● Ask the children if they can apply any of the proverbs to their life in school. Can they think of a time when too many cooks spoiled the broth? Have any of them ever judged a book by its cover?

Further support
● If the children do not understand the meaning of the proverbs, give them practical examples of where they might hear them (see examples above).

Proverbs

■ Write down the meaning of each of these proverbs.

1. When the cat's away, the mice will play.

_____

_____

2. Better late than never.

_____

_____

3. Many hands make light work.

_____

_____

4. Too many cooks spoil the broth.

_____

_____

5. Never judge a book by its cover.

_____

_____

6. A stitch in time saves nine.

_____

_____

Explaining metaphors

Objective

Y5. T2. W12.
To investigate metaphorical expressions and figures of speech from everyday life.

Guided work

1. Introduce the lesson by saying that the children will be investigating a selection of metaphorical (or idiomatic) expressions, to try to work out exactly what they mean.

2. Recall together or explain that a metaphor is used to compare two things. The writer does not say that it is *like* something else (a simile), but that it *is* something else. Use as an example the metaphor of having butterflies in your tummy. Ask the children if they know what the metaphor means (to be nervous or anxious). Draw out the understanding that you do not *literally* have butterflies inside your tummy, but you experience a fluttering sensation that can be compared to having butterflies in your tummy.

3. Ask the children if they have heard any metaphorical expressions at home, in school, or in their recent reading. Encourage them to think about expressions that people use that cannot possibly be true, for example: offering to give somebody a piece of your mind, holding your tongue and so on.

4. Give the children five minutes to have a group discussion and ask each group to feed back their favourite metaphor. Discuss each metaphor in turn, ensuring that the children appreciate that they are not literally true, but are used as a way to describe something else.

Independent work

● Based on the introductory session, decide which children will need to complete this activity in pairs or with adult support, and which children can manage independently. Explain to the children that they will be looking at six metaphorical expressions. The exercise is to try and work out what each metaphor means.

Plenary

● Review with the children what each metaphor means.
● Ask the children to work in pairs to come up with a scenario when each metaphor would be appropriate, for example: if children were arranging a surprise birthday party for a friend, they might use the expression, 'Don't let the cat out of the bag!'

Further support

● Begin a metaphor list in the classroom. Each time somebody says a metaphor, add it to the list. You will be amazed how may are used in everyday conversation.
● As homework, ask the children to find five metaphors or figures of speech from everyday language. The children may find that older generations are able to offer different examples.

Explaining metaphors

Write down the meaning of each of these metaphors.

1. Don't let the cat out of the bag!

_____

_____

2. He has his head in the clouds.

_____

_____

3. It was raining cats and dogs.

_____

_____

4. Keep your ear to the ground.

_____

_____

5. The bus flew into town.

_____

_____

6. She stabbed her friend in the back.

_____

_____

50 LITERACY HOURS FOR LESS ABLE
LEARNERS: Ages 9-11

Creating metaphors

Objective
Y6. T3. W7.
To experiment with language, for example, creating new words, similes and metaphors.

Guided work

1. Ask the children what they already know about metaphorical expressions and figures of speech. Briefly revise 'Explaining metaphors' on page 42 if appropriate. Make a list of any suggestions or explanations that are offered.

2. Remind the children that a metaphor is used to compare two things. The writer does not say that it is *like* something else (a simile) but that it *is* something else.

3. Review the meanings of several metaphors with the children, for example: *pull your socks up, sitting on the fence, butterflies in your tummy, stabbing someone in the back* and so on. Make sure the children appreciate that the metaphor is not literally true.

4. Explain to the children that they will be writing metaphors to describe a variety of different situations. Begin with the example of a child being fidgety and distracted - having ants in his pants.

5. Ask the children to discuss in pairs a metaphor that might apply to a car speeding down the road. Look for children who are struggling and pair them with more able pupils. As the children feed back, make sure the description they give is not a simile (the car was speeding *like* a bullet). Also make sure it cannot literally be true. The children might suggest, for example: *the car was flying down the road*.

6. Continue this process until the pairs become more comfortable in devising their own metaphors.

7. Show the children the six scenarios on the photocopiable sheet opposite. Model the first metaphor for the children: *The sun is shining on a beautiful day.* What might we use to describe the sun? Take suggestions from the children, for example: *a big yellow balloon, a sizzling fried egg* and so on. Select the best metaphor and add it to the sentence: *The sun is a _____ in the sky.*

Independent work

● Ask the children to work in their pairs to devise their own metaphors for each of the remaining five examples on the photocopiable sheet. Then invite each pair to spend a few minutes sharing their metaphors with the rest of the group.

Plenary

● Display a list of well-known metaphors and metaphors that the children have created. Suggest that they use metaphors in the next story they write.

Further support
● For children who struggle, provide the outline of the sentence on the photocopiable sheet. Use cloze procedure style so the children only add the metaphor.

Creating metaphors

◾ Devise your own metaphorical expressions.

Hint: make sure the expression you choose cannot literally be true.

1. The sun is shining on a beautiful day.

_____

_____

2. The wind was blowing across the playground.

_____

_____

3. Her eyes shone brightly in the lights.

_____

_____

4. The boat sailed gracefully into the harbour.

_____

_____

5. The soldier was brave in battle.

_____

_____

6. The dancers moved across the stage.

_____

_____

◾ Now try thinking of some metaphorical expressions to describe yourself.

50 LITERACY HOURS FOR LESS ABLE
LEARNERS: Ages 9–11

Perfect punctuation

Objective
Y5. T1. S6.
To understand the need for punctuation as an aid to the reader.

Guided work

1. Before the lesson begins, prepare some text for shared reading, for example: from photocopiable pages 110, 111 or 112. Avoid text that is over complicated with punctuation.

2. After a normal read through, ask the children to try to read the text excluding all of the punctuation. This will be difficult, as the children will speed up and run out of breath! Discuss with the children how this demonstrates the importance of punctuation.

3. Read the passage once more, slowly. This time ask the children to recognise each punctuation mark by marking it in the air in front of them. This process should highlight all of the punctuation in the passage to the children.

4. Discuss the different punctuation marks that occur in the passage. Look at the examples of commas, speech marks, exclamation marks and so on.

5. Then ask the children to work in groups on a different extract. Encourage them to read the passage, then to read it again without punctuation. Tell the children to annotate this piece of writing and comment on the amount and type of punctuation. *Is there a lot of speech or a list separated by commas? Are there any punctuation marks that the children do not know?*

Independent work

● Explain to the children that different punctuation marks and capital letters are missing from the passage on the photocopiable sheet opposite and that they must add them to the text. Encourage the children to keep reading the passage so that they can hear where the punctuation belongs.
● Make the children aware of the fact that, for some of the sentences, there may not be just one correct answer, so they do not need to worry if they have made different choices from those of their neighbour.

Plenary

● Use the photocopiable sheet opposite as a shared-reading text and read it through as a whole group. Encourage the children to punctuate in the air as they read. Notice and discuss any differences in the punctuation marks the children mime.

Further support
● Whenever reading a shared text, point out any new or difficult punctuation.
● Encourage the children to edit any extended writing of their own for punctuation errors by reading their piece out loud to a friend and asking the friend to check the punctuation.

Perfect punctuation

◼ Add punctuation and capital letters to this passage.

the wind whipped and a chill passed through the classroom outside
the leaves were dancing around the playground looking for an
escape would mr davies ever stop talking jon didnt think so he
usually managed to talk through an entire hour of history last thing
on a tuesday jon looked towards the gate the usual gaggle of
parents were waiting to collect their precious little children jon knew
who wouldnt be there she never was he couldnt actually remember
the last time his mum had collected him from school not that he
was bothered why should he be he was old enough to make his
own way home on the bus besides his mum didnt have time for
things like that now her two part-time cleaning jobs took up most
of her time and if she wasn't cleaning she was out with her new
boyfriend

the bell finally rang and the children started pushing their way to
the door jon pulled his coat tight around him and headed for the
bus stop
jon jon over here a voice called out jon looked round to see his
mother waving at him from amongst the group of parents her face
looked worried jon ran over why was she here what had happened

50 LITERACY HOURS FOR LESS ABLE
LEARNERS: Ages 9-11

Transforming nouns and verbs

Objective
Y5. T3. W6.
To transform words;
changing verbs to nouns,
for example, *ion*, *ism*,
ology; nouns to verbs: *ise*,
ify, *en*.

Guided work

1. Before the lesson begins, ensure that each child has scissors, card, glue, pencils, Blu-Tack, a dictionary and a copy of the photocopiable sheet opposite. Draw the table below on the board.

2. Explain to the children that they will be transforming words. Remind the children that a verb refers to an action or a state of being. Take some examples from the children and list them on the board. Also remind the children that a noun names a thing or feeling, and again list examples on the board.

3. Tell the children that, by adding suffixes, verbs can become nouns and nouns can become verbs. Use the example *light*, a noun. By adding the suffix *en*, it becomes a verb: *to lighten*. Also demonstrate using the noun *accessory* (*accessorise*) and *sympathy* (*sympathise*).

4. Then show that verbs can also be changed to nouns. The verb *to select* can be changed to a noun by adding the suffix *ion*. Other verbs which change to nouns include: *narrate* (*narrative*), *comprehend* (*comprehension*), *extend* (*extension*), *govern* (*government*) and so on.

Independent work

● Explain to the children that they will be making new words by adding suffixes, but first they need to make two spinners. They must stick their spinners onto a piece of card and then cut around them. They need to carefully thread a pencil through the centre point of the spinner. This is done by placing Blu-Tack on the table with the centre of the spinner on top, then pushing the tip of the pencil through the centre point. Show the children how to use the spinners and make a word. Write on the board the word from the spinners. Ask the children whether this word makes sense or not. Encourage children who are not sure to look the word up in the dictionary. Explain that the children will write their new words in their workbooks in table form, using the model from the board.

Further support
● If necessary, before the children cut out their spinners tell them which of the base words are nouns and which are verbs.
● Encourage the children to sound out new words as they make them, and look for spelling rules which apply when adding suffixes. Does a vowel need to be dropped before the suffix is added, for example?

Base word:	Noun or verb?	Suffix added:	New word:	Noun, verb or nonsense?
class	noun	ify	classify	verb
class	noun	ise	classise	nonsense

Plenary

● Invite the children to provide feedback on their new words. Ask them which base words could transform into verbs. Which suffixes were added for this to change? Which of the base words turned into nouns? How did this happen?

Transforming nouns and verbs

■ Glue this sheet on to card and then cut around the two spinners. Thread a pencil carefully through the centre point of each. Spin the spinners and make a word. When you add the suffix to the base word, does it make sense?

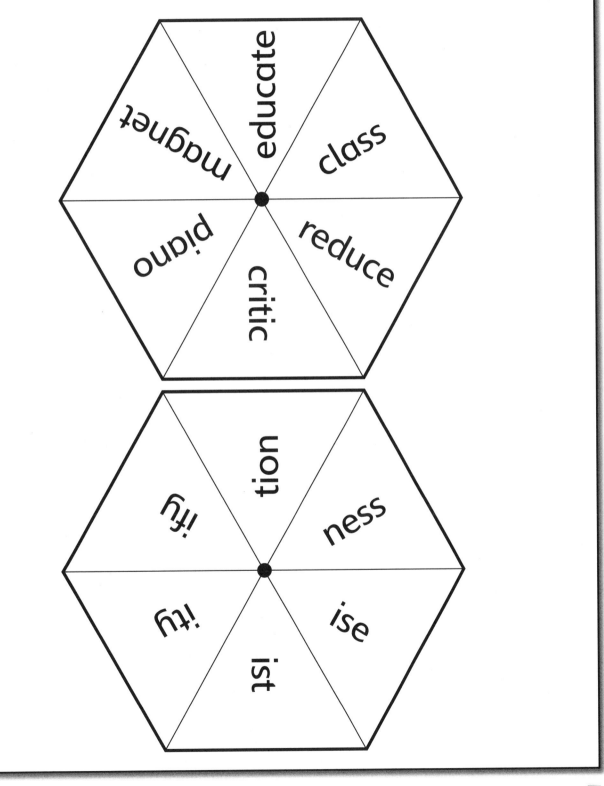

Words from other languages

Objective
Y5. T3. W8.
To identify everyday words which have been borrowed from other languages.

Guided work

1. Make sure there are plenty of dictionaries available for the children to use. Each table group will need access to glue and scissors.

2. Tell the children that they will be investigating some of the words in the English language. Explain that the English language is constantly changing. The children may have covered history topics, such as the Romans, and would recognise the influence the Roman invasion had upon the English language. Point out that many of the words in our language today come from a variety of influences and that the dictionary contains new words every year.

3. Ask the children in the class if they can think of any words that they suspect may come originally from another language.

4. Explain that the origin of a word can be checked in the dictionary. As individuals suggest words, encourage all of the children to look the word up in the dictionary, checking both the definition and the origin.

Independent work

● Explain to the children that many of our food words have also been borrowed from other languages. Ask the children if they like pizza. Can anyone tell you which language they think the word has been borrowed from? Are there any other food words that have been borrowed from other languages? Give out the photocopiable sheet opposite, and explain to the children that they must match the name of the food to the definition and the country of origin. Give the children clear instructions on how to stick their cards into their workbooks and a time limit of 20 minutes. Make sure the children look up the country of origin rather than simply guessing.

Further support
● Do not simply give easier dictionaries to children who struggle, as these may not contain origins. Provide these children with support from a more able pupil instead.
● For homework ask the children to think of more examples, perhaps from their own culture or family. Share the results of this with all the children in the class.

Plenary

● Review the cut and stick activity and give the children the answers:

Buffet	a meal of several dishes where guests help themselves	French
Spaghetti	pasta made in solid strings	Italian
Barbecue	a meal cooked outdoors on a metal grill	Spanish
Samosa	a triangular fried pastry	Indian
Chocolate	a sweet food made from roasted and ground cacao	Mexican
Cola	a drink flavoured with seeds from the cola tree	African
Hamburger	a cake of minced meat	German
Cookie	a small, sweet biscuit	American

● End the lesson by asking the children to look up several other words, as quickly as they can, to find the origin. Examples may include: *ballet, index, pyjamas, lantern* and so on.

Words from other languages

Cut out the cards and match the word with the correct definition and country of origin.

Buffet	a cake of minced meat	Spanish
Spaghetti	a triangular fried pastry	Mexican
Barbecue	a drink flavoured with seeds from the cola tree	American
Samosa	pasta made in solid strings	African
Chocolate	a small, sweet biscuit	Italian
Cola	a meal cooked outdoors on a metal grill	German
Hamburger	a meal of several dishes where guests help themselves	Indian
Cookie	a sweet food made from roasted and ground cacao	French

Different clauses

Objective
Y5. T3. S6.
To investigate clauses through identifying the main clause in a long sentence.

Guided work

1. Prepare for the lesson by writing several complex sentences on the board, for example: *After chasing the postman, the dog slept by the fire. Richard always reads a book before he goes to sleep.*

2. To start the lesson, explain that the children will be identifying the main clause in a sentence. Point out that the main clause in a sentence can stand alone, acting as a free-standing sentence. Use the example: *While at school, the children were misbehaving.* Identify the main clause in this sentence as *the children were misbehaving.* Show the children that it makes sense as a sentence on its own. Demonstrate to the children how the other clause within the sentence (*While at school*) cannot be a free-standing sentence, as it does not make sense on its own.

3. Review several other sentences with the children. If possible, underline main clauses in red and subordinate clauses in blue, as this is what the children are asked to do on the photocopiable sheet.

4. Tell the children that a clause that cannot be free-standing in a sentence is called the subordinate clause. It may help at this stage to look up the word *subordinate* in the dictionary to help the children with their understanding of the concept.

Independent work

● Give each of the children a copy of the photocopiable sheet opposite. Explain to the children that they should identify the main and subordinate clauses in the ten sentences, underlining the main clause in red and the subordinate clause in blue. Ask the children to look for the main clause in the first sentence. When they think they know what the main clause is, they should try reading that section of the sentence out loud to see if it makes sense as a complete sentence on its own. With the children, highlight *I watch television* in red and *whenever I get the chance* in blue. Tell the children to continue with the remaining sentences on their own, remembering to read each sentence quietly out loud so that they can hear the main clause.

Plenary

● Review the sentences with the children by asking them to read the whole sentence out loud, standing up during the main clause. Read through the sentences twice to give the children that chance to listen to the main clauses twice.

● End the lesson by asking the children to add to the sentence: *The children were playing....*

Further support

● It may be helpful for some of the children to concentrate on establishing the main clause in each sentence to begin with. Once they are comfortable with this, they can move on to identify the subordinate clauses.

Different clauses

I can identify the main and subordinate clauses.

█ Underline the main clause in red and the subordinate clause in blue.

1. I watch television whenever I get the chance.

2. The children played happily until it started to rain.

3. If I finish my homework I can play on my computer.

4. The dog barked before he settled down to sleep.

5. The traffic was bad so I was late.

6. After meeting my friends in the park, we go to play football.

7. Although I like it, I do not want any chocolate now.

8. Sarah's shoes were expensive but looked cheap.

9. I cannot go to the cinema tonight because I have a headache.

10. Despite his confidence, Richard did not pass his driving test.

Adapting writing

Objective
Y5. T1. S4.
To adapt writing for different readers and purposes by changing vocabulary, tone and sentence structures to suit, for example, simplifying for younger readers.

Guided work

1. Before the lesson begins, gather together a selection of story books aimed at Key Stage 1 children. Decide which story you would like rewritten for a younger audience. Fairy tales work particularly well for this activity, as in their traditional format, they are unsuitable for younger children to read independently and also, less able children will find it easier to work with a familiar story.

2. Start by telling the children the chosen story in its original format. At the end, briefly discuss the main event, the characters and the climax of the tale. Write on the board a small section of the story and ask the children to read it together.

3. Discuss the complex nature of the sentences and the vocabulary by highlighting specific examples. Do the children think this story is suitable for infant children? Ask the children to select particular words or sentences that they think younger children will find difficult.

4. Give the children some time to study the selection of story books, asking them to look out for particular features, for example: easy vocabulary, short sentences, colourful pictures and the overall length. Take feedback from the children on what makes these books seem suitable for younger children.

Independent work

● Explain to the children that they will now be adapting the story you told, and that they will be making it suitable for a younger audience. Review the storyline with the children, ensuring they have a full understanding. Give each child a copy of the photocopiable sheet opposite. Say that it breaks the story up into four parts: the introduction, the build up, the main event and the conclusion. The children must decide what information they are going to share at each part of the story and then write it in the relevant section.

● Once the children have completed their plans, they are ready to go on to write out the adapted version of the story. You will probably need to extend this work into the next session. Give the children time to edit their writing and to add illustrations. Encourage the children to create their own book with pictures and text on each page.

Further support
● Some children will find it easier to work in pairs, discussing their ideas together before completing the photocopiable sheet and the final adaptation. Make sure that both children do an equal share of writing and illustrating.

Plenary

● Share and discuss the final adaptations of the story. Ask the children to tell you what features of these versions make them suitable for younger children.

● By liaising with a Key Stage 1 class, the books can be tested out on their target audience, who could also be asked to evaluate them.

Adapting writing

Original story: _____

Written by: _____

Introduction:

> **Hint:** do we know the main characters' names and something about them? Do we know where the story is set?

Build up:

> **Hint:** have you started to describe actions? Can the reader begin to guess what could happen in the story?

Main event:

> **Hint:** has the main part of the story now happened? Is there lots of action?

Conclusion:

> **Hint:** has the story been finished off? Is there a link back to the beginning? Now think about how you might illustrate this story. What picture would go with each section of the story?

Formal language

Objective
Y6. T2. S2.
To understand features of formal official language.

Guided work

1. Have prepared in advance several examples of formal official language, preferably one example per table group. These might include application forms (passport, holiday insurance, job applications), solicitor's letters (conveyancing), letters of complaint, invitations (weddings) and so on. Examples can be selected to match the reading ability of each group. Also ensure there are plenty of dictionaries around the classroom.

2. Begin by telling the children that they are to be translators for the lesson, translating formal language to informal language. Check the children are aware of the differences between formal and informal, and ask if any of them can think of examples. (The children may also come up with other comparisons, such as dress, to help understand the concept.)

3. Write the children's suggestions on the board, modelling the format shown on the photocopiable sheet opposite. Provide some examples of your own and ask the children to translate them to informal language, for example: *smoking is prohibited, maiden name, duplicate, forename, the management cannot accept liability for loss or theft.* Tell the children that they can look up any of the words in the dictionary to check on their meaning.

Independent work

● Explain to the children that each group has been given a different example of a formal text. Invite one child from each table to hold up their text and briefly explain what they think it is. Ask the children if they can think of any similar texts. Tell the children to work together as a group to read and translate their formal text. Give each group one A3 copy of the photocopiable sheet opposite. Explain that they must find ten examples of formal words or phrases in their text to translate to informal language, and write them down on their sheet. If the children get stuck on a word, encourage them to leave that one out and select another. If a group struggles to work together, then provide each child in the group with a section of the text to analyse. Give the children 15 to 20 minutes to complete the task, supporting the groups at all times and helping out with the pronunciations of more difficult words.

Further support
● If the texts are too difficult for the children in your class, provide only one text and read it together before the lesson starts, giving the children greater experience of formal language.
● The main formal words on each text could be highlighted to help the children find the words and phrases that need to be translated.

Plenary

● Ask one child to act as spokesperson for each group to feedback on three of their ten formal phrases and their informal translations. Discuss any difficulties the children had.

Formal language

We can translate formal to informal language.

Formal language	Informal language

Our spokesperson is: _____ and our three best

formal phrases are: _____ ,

_____ and _____

Book reviews

Objectives
Y5. T1. T10.
To evaluate a book by referring to details and examples in the text.

Y5. T1. T13.
To record their ideas, reflections and predictions about a book, for example, through a reading log or journal.

Guided work

1. Read the two pieces of text on photocopiable page 108 with the children. Ask them what we call this form of writing (book reviews). See if they can identify common features in the texts. Ask them to jot down ideas that they can use to write a book review for inclusion in a class magazine.

2. Discuss their ideas and list the features they notice, for example:

- something about the main characters
- an idea about the genre
- only a little about the story
- a few details about certain parts of the story
- ending is not revealed
- descriptive words and phrases
- personal opinion – often persuading the reader how good the book is
- quotes from or references to details in the text to back up personal views.

3. Ask the children if they find the reviews useful. Do they make them want to read the book? Do they agree with the reviewer's opinion?

4. Tell the children that you would like them to help you write a brief review of *Harry Potter and the Philosopher's Stone* (or another book they are familiar with). Stress the need to include details about the story, reasons for their opinions and references to the text. Use the children's ideas to make notes on the photocopiable sheet opposite, then work to write the review together.

Independent work

- Ask the children to write a draft book review on the photocopiable sheet opposite. Tell them to choose a book that they have read recently, or ask them to write a review of the book you have just read as a group. Stress that it does not have to be a book they enjoyed, as long as they can back up their feelings. This can be discussed in pairs but written up individually. The edited book reviews could be word-processed and perhaps made into a class reading log or magazine.

Plenary

- Choose a book that you have read to the group in the past, and ask the children to discuss: what they liked about it, if anything, or what they disliked; what their favourite part was; the age group for whom they feel the book is suitable; if they would recommend it to others.

Further support
- Some children may find they have no time left to redraft, so it may be easier for them to record their book review on to a cassette rather than write it out.

Book reviews

■ Plan a book review.

Title and author:

Genre:

Ideas for opening sentence to grab the reader's attention:

Brief idea of storyline, setting and main character/s involved:	Details of parts of story and words/ phrases to quote:

Personal opinion about the story:

Myths, legends and fables

Objectives
Y5. T2. T1.
To identify and classify the features of myths, legends and fables, for example, the moral in a fable, fantastical beasts in legends.

Guided work

1. Remind the children about previous work on myths, fables and traditional tales. Ask the children to recall identifying characteristics, and to give you examples from each genre. Explain that legends are traditional tales about heroic characters like Robin Hood and King Arthur, which may be based on the truth, but which have been added to and sensationalised over the years.

2. Outline some of the typical features of a legend.

* It is a story from the past, believed to have a historical basis, but it is not possible to prove it really happened.
* It is a story continually told through generations of a particular culture.
* It may include supernatural powers or happenings.
* There is often conflict in which good characters (heroes and heroines) usually overcome evil characters (villains).
* The story and its heroes are often commemorated (for example, in books, a festival, a feast day, a statue or monument).

3. Read the extract on photocopiable page 109. Help the children with any difficult language and unusual sentence constructions. Ask the children which of the genre elements of legends they can find. Consider, for example, the characters, the narrator's style and language, the mention of an adventure and potential danger.

4. Ask the children to discuss in pairs or small groups, whether each extract on the photocopiable sheet is a myth, legend or fable.

5. Go through the activity with the children, asking them to justify their decisions. (*Answers: 1. myth, 2. fable, 3. fable, 4. legend, 5. myth, 6. legend, 7. myth, 8. fable, 9. legend, 10. fable.*)

Independent work

* Re-read photocopiable page 109 and ask the children to work in pairs to construct an oral retelling of the story. Remind them that they should include some of their own ideas, perhaps similar dramatic language and ideally an ending if possible.

Further support
* Display the elements of legends as the children work.
* Brainstorm useful names, words and phrases.

Plenary

* Ask volunteers to make up, orally, part of a story that the others could continue. It could be about Robin Hood and other members of the Outlaws, and their confrontations with the Sheriff of Nottingham and his men.

Myths, legends and fables

▪ Identify whether each of these extracts is from a myth, legend or fable.

1. A monster with four snarling heads appeared from the smoking volcano and flew on bat-like wings towards our hero.

_____

2. Then the hen sat down and cried with disappointment. The moral of the story is: Do not count your chickens before they are hatched.

_____

3. So the tortoise challenged the hare to a race and the hare accepted, laughing. The hare set off at a cracking speed while the tortoise plodded along in his own slow way. But the hare soon became tired and sat behind a tree to doze.

_____

4. Suddenly a shining sword, studded in jewels, started to emerge from the centre of the lake and eventually a knight's hand appeared from the calm water holding it high. That sword was Excalibur.

_____

5. Long, long ago and far away the gods became angry with the people for wasting precious rainwater. The gods decided to punish the people by sending a terrible drought.

_____

6. Joan of Arc was no ordinary French girl. Born in 1412, at the time of much fighting in France, this very young woman led a French army to many victories.

_____

7. Jason and the Argonauts set sail on the quest for the Golden Fleece. They were to encounter many strange creatures and monsters during the voyage as well as being confronted with numerous impossible challenges.

_____

8. There was once a fox that really wanted some grapes that he had seen hanging from the highest branch of a vine. 'I'm going to get those grapes if it's the last thing I do!' he said loudly.

_____

9. So, as a punishment, William Tell was given the task of shooting an apple which was put on his son's head.

_____

10. The lion lay on the floor quivering next to the triumphant and victorious mouse. This just goes to prove strength is not always physical power.

_____

50 LITERACY HOURS FOR LESS ABLE LEARNERS: Ages 9-11

Point of view

Objective

Y5. T2. T8.

To distinguish between the author and the narrator, investigating narrative viewpoint and the treatment of different characters.

Guided work

1. Read photocopiable page 110 with the children. Point out that Michael Morpurgo is the *author*, the writer of the story. Then tell them that authors can write their stories in different styles and choose to tell the story from different points of view. The voice telling the story is the *narrator*. Explain that this voice does not necessarily take the same viewpoint as the author might personally hold.

2. Read the text again and ask the children to identify who is telling the story. Is it a character in the story? If so, can they work out which one? Or is it someone from outside the action? Help the children to see that the use of *I, we, me* and *my* (first person) tells us that the narrator is a character in the story and that the use of *he, she* and *they* (third person) indicates the narrator is external to the story.

3. Once the children have identified that a character is telling the story, ask them to read the extract again. Discuss what they have found out about that character and how he feels about anyone else in the story. Look at words such as *saviour* and *tenderly* and how the narrator's recovery causes Kensuke to smile for the first time. Explain how an external narrator can see, know and comment on all the action – he/she is omniscient, or all-seeing, but a character-narrator can only narrate what they witness or hear about from another character. See if the children can also identify Stella as an animal rather than a person (Michael's dog).

4. Read photocopiable pages 111 and 112 in turn, pointing out the name of the author, and repeating the identification of the narrator.

Independent work

● Give the children a copy of the photocopiable sheet opposite and ask them to read each extract in turn and identify the narrator.
● To challenge the children further, you could ask them to re-read the extracts in which a character narrates the story and write about what they have learned about that character.

Further support

● Support children with difficult vocabulary and focus on differentiating between first- and third-person narrators rather than between author and narrator. Help them to imagine the same viewpoint as the narrator.

Plenary

● Discuss how the children decided who was the narrator in the extracts, for example: the use of first- or third-person words or the long timescale in the third extract. See if the children can name any of the characters/narrators. In the second extract, it could be either a friend of Ali and Raj recalling an event or, as the 'omniscient', formal style would suggest, an external narrator. Emphasise the difference between the author and the narrator – the narrator's point of view is not necessarily that of the author.

Point of view

◼ Read each of these story extracts and decide whether the narrator is external or a character within the story. Note your decision on the line. If possible, include the name of the character who is telling the story.

1. The weather was sunny but I felt cloudy inside. I had just arrived for a two-week stay with my grumpy old Aunt Freda.

'Darling Ben!' Aunt said as I got out of the car. 'How lovely to see you!' she said with a forced grin on her face. 'You will take off those dirty shoes before you come, in won't you?'

_____

_____

3. A wisp of wind gently fluttered the tattered, grubby net curtains that hung at the window. The abandoned old house had been empty, or almost empty, for over half a century. It was 'almost empty' as the ghost of Grizzly Gertrude had lingered here ever since that day, fifty-six years ago, when she had died in this very bedroom.

_____

_____

2. Ali and Raj disappeared over the edge of the cliff and slithered down the chalky rock. It was their first day at the caravan park near Sandytown and they were determined to explore every centimetre of the place. Unfortunately, they had not stopped to consider how high tide might affect this part of the coastline.

_____

_____

4. 'I don't want to go!' I screamed as Mum tried to force me into my coat.

'But you know you'll enjoy it once you get there,' said Mum. 'But Tam will be going and last time we met we had a big row,' I argued. 'Mel, you need to forget all about that and the two of you need to make up,' said Mum. 'So get your coat on, now!'

_____

_____

Changing the point of view

Guided work

1. Read photocopiable page 110 with the children and establish that the story is being told by one of the characters. If the children do not know the story, tell them that the narrator is Michael, shipwrecked on a desert island just before his twelfth birthday. He soon realises that there is someone else on the island who, although he gives Michael food and drink, will not let him swim in the sea or light a fire to try to attract rescue.

2. Read the extract again and ask the children to consider how the story would be different if told from the point of view of Kensuke. The discussion may cover, for example, why Kensuke kept Michael 'captive', how Kensuke felt and what he was thinking, rather than how Michael felt and thought.

3. Display the extract (ideally on an interactive whiteboard) and ask the children to help you rewrite the first paragraph from Kensuke's point of view. Work through the paragraph a sentence at a time, asking the children to think of themselves as Kensuke and imagine what he would see, hear and feel. The paragraph could be something like:

> The boy lay very still, but his eyes roamed around my cave. He seemed to be trying to talk, but I could barely hear a whisper from his lips. His eyes suddenly looked frightened, as though he had remembered the terrible incident with the jellyfish. I bent over him and wiped his forehead gently. 'You better now,' I said. 'My name Kensuke. You better now.' Then the dog came over and put its nose into the boy's ear.

Independent work

● Give the children a copy of the photocopiable sheet opposite and read the extract with them. Establish who is telling the story. Tell the children that you now want them to rewrite the extract from the point of view of Jaz. Briefly discuss this viewpoint, asking them, for example: *Did Jaz know who had put the sand in the bag? How does Jaz feel about being told off for something he hasn't done? What does Jaz think about Greg if he knows it was Greg that put the sand in the bag?* Encourage the children to write their first draft under the extract, redraft and then continue the story if they have time.

Plenary

● Ask for volunteers to read their extract from Jaz's point of view and then ask if anyone would like to retell the paragraph as an external narrator, using the viewpoint of someone not involved in the action.

Changing the point of view

◢ Rewrite this extract from Jaz's point of view.

It was me, Greg Whiteham, that was really responsible for the chaos. I was the one

who had moved Roy's bag, filled it full of sand and put it back on his peg, but it was

Jaz that was now being blamed. I stood listening to Mr Williams shouting with rage

at Jaz but I just couldn't own up – that is until I saw the first tear start to roll down

poor Jaz's cheek.

Final Draft:

50 LITERACY HOURS FOR LESS ABLE
LEARNERS: Ages 9-11

Different genres

Objective
Y5. T2. T9.

To investigate the features of different fiction genres, for example, science fiction, adventure, discussing the appeal of popular fiction.

Guided work

1. Display this list as a poster and read it through:

> **Genre** distinguishes different types of writing, each with specific characteristics that relate to reader interest area. These are some of the common fiction genres:
>
> **Science fiction** - an imaginative story often set in the future, involving space travel or scientific gadgets.
> **Adventure** - an exciting tale, often involving a journey, which, although usually exaggerated, could be true.
> **Mystery/horror** - a story about something unexplained or secret, usually with an atmosphere that is spine chilling or spooky.
> **Historical** - a story set at some point in the past, this could be the recent past or distant past.
> **Fantasy** - a story often set in an imaginary place or time, with fantastical creatures and magical events.
> **Traditional tales** - stories which have been handed down for generations of a particular culture.
> **Humorous/funny stories** - stories to make us laugh.

2. Discuss the different genres and which ones individuals like or dislike and why. What is the appeal about one genre rather than another? What makes certain books appeal more than others? Ask the children which books and films they would include in some of the categories. Encourage them to explain why they put them in a particular category.

3. Read examples from photocopiable pages 109 to 114 and ask the children to identify the genres. Ask them to find clues in the text that suggest the genre they have chosen. Remind the children that some extracts could be included in a couple of the genres.

4. Discuss their decisions as a whole group and whether the different groups used the same clues to decide upon the genre in each case.

Independent work

● Ask the children to read each extract on the photocopiable sheet opposite in turn and identify the genre. Then ask the children to identify key words and phrases that helped them decide.

Plenary

● Choose one of the extracts from the activity, and do a short piece of shared writing work with the children to rewrite the extract into a different genre.

Further support
● Some children may need adult support in order to read the extracts in the activity before they can write the answers.
● If necessary, help individuals to compare the extracts with books they know or extracts shared in the lesson to notice similarities.

Different genres

■ Identify and write the genre of each of these short extracts from stories.
■ Then, on a separate sheet, write the key words and phrases that give the clues as to the genre.

1. Hattie felt herself falling deeper and deeper down the hole until eventually she hit the bottom with a bounce! She had landed on what appeared to be a bouncy castle. She sat up and looked around. She seemed to be in a town full of bouncy castles, all vivid colours and crazy shapes like the one she'd seen at the village fair.

_____

2. The sleek craft was hovering just above the town. Then, on the beam of green light that suddenly shone into the empty car park, strange little beings began gliding down to Earth.

_____

3. Kye crept round the creaky old door and disappeared into the castle. There was a weird scent in the air, fusty and dank. He suddenly got the distinct impression he was not alone – that someone, or something, was watching him.

_____

4. As daylight turned to dusk Sal and Dan became nervous and frightened. They had no idea where they were or what had happened to the rest of the group. They must have taken a wrong turn way back at that fork in the path and were now a long way from where they had pitched the tent that morning.

_____

5. Emily lit the night candle by holding it carefully over the oil lamp. She then said goodnight to her Mama and Papa and, holding her long skirts in one hand and the candlestick in the other, she climbed the old oak staircase. She was looking forward to her cosy bed from which Mary, the maid, had just removed the warming pan full of hot coals.

_____

50 LITERACY HOURS FOR LESS ABLE
LEARNERS: Ages 9-11

Literal and figurative

Objective
Y5. T2. T10.
To understand the differences between literal and figurative language.

Guided work

1. Talk through this information with the children:

> **Literal language** uses only accurate detail of the subject and uses words in their usual, basic sense, for example: *The engine made a purring noise.*
>
> **Figurative language** uses metaphors or similes to create a particular impression or mood. The description uses unusual meanings of words and is exaggerated or poetic. Two of the most common forms of figurative language are similes and metaphors.
>
> **Similes** compare two different things using the word *like* or *as*, for example: *The noise from the engine was like a cat's purr.*
>
> **Metaphors** are like similes, but do not use *like* or *as*; they usually describe something as if it were really something else, for example: *The engine purred softly.*

2. Discuss the difference between literal and figurative language and identify the two kinds of figurative language listed. Ask the children if they can think of any similes or metaphors. They may give examples like: *As fast as a speeding bullet* or *Raining cats and dogs*. Tell them that figurative language is most often used in fiction and poetry rather than non-fiction. Use photocopiable page 112 to point out a few examples of figurative language (for example, *The people of Ledsham flowed..., Thomas Kempe made a wall of air, as insistent as a wave at sea...*), and photocopiable page 116 (for example, *He stands there like the stump of a tree, with a forest of arms around*).

Independent work

● Tell the children to read the passage on the photocopiable sheet opposite. Ask them to choose the most appropriate phrase for each space in the text and identify the phrase as simile, metaphor or literal. Go through the first one completed as an example. The children could work in pairs to discuss the phrases.

Plenary

● Display the extract on photocopiable page 112 and ask the children if they can think of any similes or metaphors that could be introduced into the text, for example: *as cold as ice* could be added to make the phrase, *but James could feel him as cold as ice nonetheless.*

Further support
● This is a difficult concept and some children may need adult support to distinguish the language types. Use the definitions and remind them of the examples given at the beginning of the lesson.

Literal and figurative

◼ Write the most appropriate phrase into each space in this text. Then mark it as **simile**, **metaphor** or **literal** in the brackets. The first one has been done for you.

Simon ran *as fast as the wind* [*simile*]. His heart was _____

[_____]. He was soaking wet because it was

_____ [_____]. By the time he reached the station

the train had gone. Simon watched it chug along the track that

_____ [_____]. _____

[_____] he stared down the line. He turned around and started for home,

with water dripping _____ [_____]. As he stepped

into the kitchen his Mum gasped _____ [_____].

'You're just _____!' [_____] she exclaimed. 'Take

those wet things off immediately and I'll go and run you

_____. [_____] We'll have you

_____ [_____] in no time!'

---

as if sucked dry of all air　　**raining cats and dogs**

snaked down the valley　　**beating loudly in his chest**

a nice hot bath　　**as fast as the wind**　　**Like a deserted dog**

as warm as toast　　**from every part of his body**　　**a drowned rat**

50 LITERACY HOURS FOR LESS ABLE LEARNERS: Ages 9-11

Additional dialogue

Objective
Y5. T3. T9.
To write in the style of the author, for example, writing additional dialogue.

Guided work

1. Remind the children of some key points about dialogue:

- It can add detail and interest into stories.
- It involves a conversation between two or more people.
- The words people say are presented within speech marks.
- Other punctuation is used differently when speech is written.
- When a different person speaks, it is written on a new line.

2. Display photocopiable page 111 and read it through with the children. Pay particular attention to the dialogue.

3. Ask the children to work in groups of three and imagine they are listening to the rest of the conversation between the children and the bird. Ask them to think about: how the bird would respond to finding out that Robert had put the egg in the fire, how the conversation might continue, and how it would end. Encourage the children to look at the words the characters use and then continue their conversation, making sure that they continue to give the characters their own individual style of speaking, and making the dialogue fit in with the style of the book's author, E Nesbit.

4. When they have had some time to do this, invite one of the groups to act out their conversation or record it on audio or video tape. Then ask them to repeat it slowly as you record part of the dialogue on the board, using the appropriate punctuation.

5. Re-read the extract, including the new dialogue. Consider how well it fits and if the author's style has been maintained.

Independent work

- Read the extract on the photocopiable sheet opposite with the children to make sure that they understand what is happening in the text. Ask them to brainstorm with a partner what details could be included as dialogue to add an ending to this situation. Then ask them to write the end of the story, using mainly dialogue between the three characters. Remind them to maintain the writing style of the author.

Plenary

- Display a different extract from the back of this book and ask the children to suggest some dialogue in the same way.
- Ask the children to make up some more unusual dialogue (perhaps between a mother and a toddler, people speaking a local dialect or people speaking in rap).

Further support
- Display examples of written dialogue to help with the appropriate layout and punctuation.
- The dialogue the children devise could be recorded on to cassette before writing it.

Additional dialogue

◀ Read the extract below, then add some dialogue to give more detail about the situation.

◀ Brainstorm some ideas and jot them in the box below before adding your dialogue to continue the text. Consider: what does Jake find? Is it valuable? What will the children do about it? Will Rosie and Sean continue to argue?

[ ]

Jake, with his best friend Sean and Sean's little sister, Rosie, were on their way back from the park. As usual Sean and Rosie were arguing.

'Mum will be cross,' said Rosie. 'She said we must be back for tea at six o'clock.'

'Oh shut up, pest, or I won't let you come with us again,' warned Sean.

'But I'm hungry,' moaned Rosie. 'It's nearly 7 o'clock!'

Jake had just about had enough of both of them. 'Listen you two,' he said. 'If you don't stop arguing I'll...' But something glinting brightly on the ground made Jake stop dead in his tracks. 'Look at that!' he continued, bending down to pick up the...

[ ]

Writing a synopsis

Objectives

Y6. T1. T8.
To summarise a passage, chapter or text in a specified number of words.

Y6. T3. T10.
To write a brief synopsis of a text, for example, for back cover blurb.

Guided work

1. Revise work on book reviews and persuasive writing.

2. Display photocopiable page 115 and read the blurb for *The Thieves of Ostia* together. Ask the children where they might find a piece of writing like this and if they know what it is called, or tell them that it is a blurb and is usually found on the back cover of a book (if possible show them some examples). Ask them why it is there and what can be found out about a book from reading it. (It tells the reader what sort of book it is and, in the case of fiction, a little about the story.) Tell them that a blurb never gives away the ending of the story as it is written to tantalise the reader into wanting to read the book. Blurbs, in contrast to synopses, sometimes focus on one significant or intriguing early part of the plot. Tell the children that they are going to write a blurb, which could be word-processed and perhaps displayed in the school or class library.

3. Read the other blurb on photocopiable page 115 and discuss it in the same way.

4. Now read the synopsis with the group. Tell them that this is a synopsis of the same story. Ask the children if they can see a difference between this and the blurb, or tell them that this synopsis briefly retells the whole story, whereas a blurb just hints at the story. Both are short pieces of writing, which include very little detail. Stress that a synopsis is a 'straight' retelling of the story whereas a blurb is persuasive, to try to influence the reader into reading the whole book. Discuss the similarities and differences between the blurb and the synopsis of *The Hodgeheg*.

Independent work

● Give the children a copy of the photocopiable sheet opposite and ask them to work with a partner editing this synopsis into a briefer one, making it only 100 words long. Remind them that their synopsis should still outline the story.

● Display the blurbs on photocopiable page 115 and read them again to the group. Ask them to use the synopsis that they have just worked on, add a persuasive element and omit the ending to write a blurb of *James and the Giant Peach*.

Plenary

● Ask children to write a brief synopsis of a book that they have just read, omitting to mention the title and author. Ask some volunteers to read theirs out for the rest of the group to work out which book is being described.

Further support

● Encourage the children to read their first attempt to a partner to get some feedback about the accuracy of the synopsis or persuasiveness of the blurb.

Writing a synopsis

■ Edit this text to make a synopsis of no more than 100 words. Underline the most important points and then write your synopsis on a separate sheet.

James and the Giant Peach by Roald Dahl is about a little boy who, when orphaned, goes to live with two horrible mean aunts, Aunt Spiker and Aunt Sponge, on the top of a remote hill. They make poor James's life a misery, doing all their hard work, until one magical day when the old peach tree, which has never produced any fruit before, grows an enormous peach. The two old women see this as an opportunity to make plenty of money, by charging people to come and see the gigantic peach, but poor James is locked away from all the fun. But that night James goes out to the tree and finds a large hole in the side of the peach, and so crawls in to investigate. Inside he finds six unusually large creatures: Grasshopper, Spider, Ladybird, Centipede, Earthworm and Silkworm.

During the night, the peach falls from the tree and starts to roll down the hill, gathering momentum rapidly, rolling right over the two aunts. Eventually the peach rolls into the sea and the adventure begins for James and his six new friends. First they are attacked by sharks but, by using Earthworm as bait, they attract seagulls which they lasso with Silkworm's thread to pull them out of danger. The peach, now floating through the air, is then attacked by Cloud-Men, but the adventurers manage to escape and find land in the form of America – landing on the spike at the top of the Empire State Building. James and his friends are rescued safe and sound and become famous heroes.

Flashback!

Objective
Y6. T2. T11.
To write own story using, for example, flashbacks or a story within a story to convey the passing of time.

Guided work

1. Display photocopiable page 110 and read it with the children. Ask them to identify particular words and phrases that indicate how the author has shown the passing of time. Underline these (for example, *I remembered* in the first paragraph, and *for how many days* in the third). Ask the children if they think the incident with the jellyfish happened several years, weeks or days ago and why they think this. What hints are given in the extract that there is a flashback – someone retelling something that has already happened, a recount?

2. Repeat the process using photocopiable page 113. Discuss the different style that is used to indicate the flashback in *Time Trap* in contrast to *Kensuke's Kingdom*. (In *Time Trap*, the narrator speaks directly to the reader, asking, for example, *do you remember?* and then gives a recap of the story so far. In *Kensuke's Kingdom* the narrator is recalling events that have already happened as he begins to remember things.) Remind the children that flashbacks are a useful tool in writing to tell the reader how a past event has influenced the current story.

3. Brainstorm words and phrases which could introduce a flashback or indicate time and the passing of time, making a list of these on the whiteboard, for example: *The first time I ever..., I remember when..., This happened several years ago.*

4. Remind the children about the different types of story in which flashbacks might be significant (a diary, a ship's log, a recount, a time machine, memories, and a story within a story).

Independent work

● Ask the children to use the photocopiable sheet opposite to plan a story that includes a flashback or a story from the past within the story. Tell them to discuss some ideas with a partner before writing their own story plan. The children could write about a memory (beginning *I remember...*, for example), diary entries, imagining the past from reading a history book, or travelling in a time machine.

Further support
● Display the chart of time connectives you made to help the children to express the passing of time and sequence of events. Ask for suggestions to add to the list.

Plenary

● Play a game of verbal 'Consequences' where the first child starts a story about a time machine and the rest of the group take turns in adding to the story to go forward and backwards in time, using time connectives wherever possible (avoiding *and then*!) For example: *This morning I..., The year was 1573..., When I landed I was surrounded by Roman soldiers..., I hurtled through time..., finding myself looking at fierce dinosaurs....*

Flashback!

Narrator: first person account, explain who is telling the story	
Setting: is the setting the same in the flashback, or is it different? How long ago did the events in the flashback take place?	
First paragraph: using information from the two sections above and introducing the main story	
Flashback: how the flashback is achieved (for example, *memories, time travel, dream sequence, a story within a story*). What the flashback shows – what happens in it Sequence of events including time connectives, (for example, *I remember, in the beginning, after breakfast, at dusk*) How will the story move back to main story and time?	
Story ending (if you have time): conclusion to main story	

The poet's style

Objective
Y5. T1. T6.
To read a number of poems by significant poets and identify what is distinctive about the style or content of their poems.

Guided work

1. Divide the children into four groups and give one group a copy of photocopiable page 118, the second group page 119, the third group page 120 and the fourth group page 121. Ask the children to read the poems, helping them out with difficult language as necessary, and try to answer these questions:

* If you have more than one poem, have the titles got anything in common?
* Who has written each poem?
* If you have more than one poem, what do they have in common?
* Do the poems rhyme? If any of the poems rhyme, what is the pattern? For example, AABAABCA.
* Do any of the poems have rhythm?
* Does the poem have short lines, long lines or a mixture?
* Is the vocabulary modern or old-fashioned?
* Is there a theme across the poems or verses, or not?
* How does the language help you to understand the poem?
* Do you like or dislike the poem? Why?

2. Select a child in each group to be the scribe to jot down ideas.

3. Ask the first group to sit with the third group and the second group to sit with the fourth group. Ask them to share their poems and talk through their notes with the group they have joined.

4. Ask the children to compare the sets of poems.

5. Join back together as a whole group and discuss the children's finding and ideas. These might include that all the haikus have three lines in them and do not rhyme; all the verses in 'Maggie and the Dinosaur', except the first verse, have four lines and rhyme with the pattern ABCB (the first verse rhymes ABCBDB).

Further support
* Some children will need adult help and support to read and understand the poems and to compare and contrast them. Encourage them to use the list of questions from the lesson to help with this process.
* When giving the children a partner, choose a child who is more able to work with a child who is a little less able.

Independent work

* Give the children photocopiable pages 116 and 117 and the activity opposite. Encourage the children to work in pairs, reading the poems and using the questions or statements above to discuss the four poems and the styles of the two poets. Then ask the children to work individually to record their ideas on the evaluation sheet.

Plenary

* Ask for volunteers to share one or two of their ideas about the similarities and differences in the style of the poems by the two poets. Discuss which style of poetry the children prefer and why.

The poet's style

◼ Discuss and evaluate the styles of the two poets.

Title of the poem				
Poet				
What is the poem about?				
Does the poem have rhyme?				
What rhyming pattern is used? (For example: A, B, A, B)				
Does the poem have rhythm?				
Is the language similar to any of the other poems?				
Do you like or dislike the poem? Why?				
What do the two poems tell you about the poet's style				

50 LITERACY HOURS FOR LESS ABLE
LEARNERS: Ages 9-11

Writing a rap

Objectives

Y5. T2. T6.

To understand terms which describe different kinds of poems, for example, ballad, sonnet, rap, elegy, narrative poem, and to identify typical features.

Y5. T2. T12.

To use the structures of poems read to write extensions based on these, for example, additional verses, or substituting own words and ideas.

Guided work

1. Share photocopiable pages 118 and 119 and the poem 'Cat's Funeral' on page 117 with the children. Read each poem and identify the type of poem by its typical characteristics. For example:

> • 'Write-A-Rap Rap' is a rap, a form of oral poetry with strong rhythm and rapid pace, and often rhyme. It is originally associated with Caribbean cultures, but has now been widely adopted into many other cultures and is often used in modern music. (Beware as many musical raps the children may know contain extremely offensive language!)
> • 'Maggie and the Dinosaur' tells a story and is therefore called a narrative poem. A ballad is a type of narrative poem (or song) characterised by short, regular verses and regular rhyme.
> • 'Cat's Funeral' is an example of an elegy, a poem or song which is a lament, a song of grief, usually for someone or something which has died.

2. Ask the children which of the poems they like and why. Encourage them to refer to the different aspects of the poems as well as the language used and the images created. Then focus the discussion on 'Write-A-Rap Rap' and tell the children that they are going to help you write a rap about food.

3. Recall the characteristics of rap, and use the photocopiable sheet opposite to jot down the children's ideas for images, words and phrases.

4. Then use the notes to draft a rap together, or use the one given on the photocopiable sheet.

Independent work

• Give the children the photocopiable sheet opposite and encourage them to plan two or three more verses to 'Food Rap', either individually or in pairs. Remind them to notice and keep to the rhythm and rhyme scheme. Then ask the children to write the extra verses using their planning notes. If appropriate, encourage them to word-process and edit the poem on screen.

Plenary

• Ask the children to get into small groups and practise some of their verses to perform in front of the rest of the group or class. They could add background music and rhythms, actions and costumes to liven up the performance.

Further support

• Remind the children to re-read the verses given, perhaps quietly out loud, to hear and feel the rhythm and notice the rhyme.

• Encourage the children to keep stopping and trying to say their rap while quietly clapping the rhythm to help them get the sounds right, as raps are meant to be oral poems.

Writing a rap

◼ Read the poem below, then complete this organiser to help plan additional verses to the rap.

Words and phrases to include: types of food, foods you enjoy or foods you hate, what food tastes like, healthy food, fun food

Pairs of rhyming words: (for example, *fish/dish, chocs/box, greens/beans*)

Food Rap

Well, we can write a rap,
With a rhythm we can clap.
We can write about food,
'Cos we're really in the mood.

Now we all love to eat,
When we're chewing on our meat.
But chips are the best,
So have one, be my guest!

Narrative poems

Objectives

Y5. T2. T6.

To understand terms which describe different kinds of poems, for example, ballad, sonnet, rap, elegy, narrative poem, and to identify typical features.

Y5. T2. T12.

To use the structures of poems read to write extensions based on these, for example, additional verses, or substituting own words and ideas.

Guided work

1. Read the poem on photocopiable page 119 with the children. Ask them what this type of poem is called (a narrative poem). Why is this name appropriate? (Because it tells a story.)

2. Read the poem again and then ask the children to think about the following questions with a partner or in a small group:

- How is the first verse different from the others?
- What happens in the poem?
- Does the poem rhyme? If so, what rhyming pattern is used? Is the same rhyming pattern used throughout the poem? (Most of the poem rhymes in an ABCB pattern apart from the first verse, with six lines, which has a pattern of ABCBDB. Also in the fifth verse, *lift* and *fit* do not rhyme, and in the eighth verse, *hall* does not rhyme with *door*. The sixth verse changes the rhyme by having a plural on *stairs*.)

3. Discuss with the children the features of a narrative poem, asking them how the poem compares to a story in terms of plot, structure, characterisation and setting.

4. Brainstorm ideas for adding to this narrative poem, or ask the children to do this in small groups and then discuss their ideas as a whole group. What other adventures could Maggie have with the dinosaur? (They could go to watch a game of football, visit Maggie's house, travel on a train or bus, go to find the dinosaur's 'relatives' in the rocks, on the beach and so on.)

Independent work

- Give the children a copy of the photocopiable sheet opposite and a copy of 'Maggie and the Dinosaur' and encourage them to plan a few more verses to continue the story with another little adventure for the two characters. Ask the children to jot down some ideas for useful words and phrases as well as rhyming words, either individually or in pairs, then to write their own extra verses using their planning. Remind them to try to write in the same style as the original poem. If possible let them word-process and edit their verses.

Plenary

- Practise the poem 'Maggie and the Dinosaur', with or without one of the children's extensions of the poem, as a piece of performance poetry. Read the poem as a group with a volunteer as the voice of the dinosaur in the second, tenth and twelfth verses and a small group of children as the 'people' in the seventh verse.

Further support

- Encourage the children to keep reading a verse of the original and then a verse they have written to make sure the style of the original is evident in the new verses of the poem. They could read them to a partner and ask for feedback.

Narrative poems

◼ Complete this organiser to plan extra verses for
'Maggie and the Dinosaur'.

Ideas for a new adventure for Maggie and the dinosaur:

Useful words and phrases: description of the dinosaur and Maggie,
description of a different setting, action words – what the dinosaur does
and how he moves and so on

Possible pairs of rhyming words:

Humorous verse

Objective
Y6. T2. T4.
To investigate humorous verse: how poets play with meanings; nonsense words and how meaning can be made of them; where the appeal lies.

Guided work

1. Share photocopiable page 120 with the children. Read each poem in turn and ask the children if they found it funny and, if so, which aspects in particular (for example, words spelled wrongly, comical words, word play, silly images created and so on).

2. As you discuss the poem 'Ettykett', draw the children's attention to the spelling of the title (the phonetic spelling of *etiquette*) and talk about the meaning of the word (a code of conduct on how we should behave). Draw the children's attention to the rhyming words at the end of the fourth line in each verse, and ask what these nonsense words might mean and why the poet has used them. Ask them why they think this poem is classed as a nonsense or humorous poem.

3. While discussing the poem 'I Saw a Jolly Hunter', include the idea that this poem tells a story but has a twist at the end, because the hunter ends up dead rather than the hare he is trying to shoot. Point out the frequent use of the word *jolly* and if necessary explain that, traditionally, the country hunters were upper class and spoke very correctly. They had a reputation for using phrases like *jolly good*. Ask them why they think this poem is a nonsense or humorous poem.

4. When discussing 'Where Teachers Keep Their Pets', look at the unusual rhyming pattern which rhymes the teacher's name near the beginning of the first line with the ends of the first and second lines – apart from in the last verse! Can the children tell you why they think the poet has written this verse differently? Ask the children why they think this poem is funny. Ask if they can think of any other verses they could add to this poem.

Further support
● By reading the poem aloud, children will probably be able to identify any nonsense words. Then read the poem again, asking the children to think about what is happening in the poem, so they can consider what the nonsense word might mean.
● A more capable child could be paired with a less able one for them to work together.

Independent/guided work
● Give the children a copy of photocopiable sheet opposite and ask them to read each verse and write what they think the poet meant by the word underlined and why they think this. Give them a made-up example, such as: in the line, *The dog went flubberly and sank to the ground*, the word *flubberly* sounds a bit like rubbery and, as the dog fell to the ground, this might be what is meant by this nonsense word. The activity could be carried out in pairs or individually. If possible, ask the children to replace the nonsense word with a similar-sounding word or rhyme.

Plenary
● Ask the children to make up a nonsense word and use it in a sentence. The rest of the children can guess what the word means – The children were *gribbling* because they had to work very hard.

Humorous verse

■ Read these verses and substitute appropriate words instead of the nonsense words that are underlined.

The witch cast her spell

With a swish and <u>cazoose</u>.

And the horse began dancing

A waltz with the moose.

Whilst out on a raid

The <u>creely</u> old fox,

Put his feet in a puddle

And lost both his <u>frocks</u>.

The <u>grib</u> and the <u>grobble</u>

Set off with a wobble,

Pedalling down the lane.

But try as they might

To cover their <u>klight</u>

Their faces were lit up with pain.

The gardener grew flowers –

Self-raising and plain.

He sowed them and hoed them

And watched while they <u>chrew</u>.

Nothing could stop the terrible din,

As the <u>flopilons</u> bunny opened the bin.

And out <u>flumped</u> old foxy hiding within,

And deafened the bunny who started to <u>glin</u>.

Haiku poetry

Guided work

1. Clap the syllables as you say, *My name is (for example, Mrs Coyne).* Ask the children to clap as you repeat it. Then ask them to take turns saying, *My name is _____,* while clapping.

2. Tell the children that they are clapping the syllables in the words, and that syllables are the beats.

3. Tell them that a haiku is a Japanese form of poetry written in three lines using 17 syllables in the pattern: five on the first line, seven on the second line and five again on the third line.

4. Display photocopiable page 121 and read each poem discussing them with the children, pointing out that most of the poems are about the seasons, weather or nature. The poems create mental images because of the descriptive words used. Discuss what each haiku is about, then read each poem again, clapping the syllables while the children count five-seven-five.

5. Tell the children that haikus are often written about the seasons or months, and then brainstorm some useful words and phrases on this theme. As you write the children's suggestions, ask them to work out the number of syllables and mark them over the words and phrases using a comma for each.

6. Draw a couple of boxes, like the ones on the photocopiable activity opposite, and model writing a haiku. You could do something like:

January's bleak

Blowing an icy chill wind

Freezing cold winter

Independent work

● Hand out the photocopiable activity and tell the children that they are going to write part of a haiku calendar, writing about four consecutive months of the year. Explain that the activity sheet has little marks (commas) to help them work out the number of syllables they need in each line and two boxes to help them perfect each haiku.

Plenary

● Ask for a few volunteers to read out their haikus. Let each child share their poem first, then ask them to read it out again while the rest of the group clap out the syllables.

Haiku poetry

■ Use the boxes below to help you write part of a haiku calendar. Use the commas to help you work out the number of syllables each word needs.

First Attempt	Second Attempt	Final Haiku
, , , , ,	, , , , ,	
, , , , , , ,	, , , , , , ,	
, , , , ,	, , , , ,	

First Attempt	Second Attempt	Final Haiku
, , , , ,	, , , , ,	
, , , , , , ,	, , , , , , ,	
, , , , ,	, , , , ,	

First Attempt	Second Attempt	Final Haiku
, , , , ,	, , , , ,	
, , , , , , ,	, , , , , , ,	
, , , , ,	, , , , ,	

First Attempt	Second Attempt	Final Haiku
, , , , ,	, , , , ,	
, , , , , , ,	, , , , , , ,	
, , , , ,	, , , , ,	

A playscript

Objective
Y5. T1. T18.
To write own playscript, applying conventions learned from reading; including production notes.

Guided work

1. Display photocopiable page 109 and read it with the children. Tell them that you are going write this story as a playscript.

2. Remind the children about previous work on playscripts and discuss the following points.

> ● A playscript is written mainly as dialogue and the speaker is indicated in the margin.
> ● The story is told through the dialogue, so it is important that this gives the audience details about the plot.
> ● In a playscript, stage directions tell the actors how to behave and where to move. This also helps to tell the story, but the audience only sees this by watching the action on stage.

3. Brainstorm what other things would need to be considered before a playscript could be produced as a play (scenery and props, costumes, lighting, music, sound effects). These *production notes* tell the director and production team how to present the play.

4. Read through 'How Little John Came to the Greenwood', picking out aspects of the text that would inform the production notes of a playscript. This might include the fact that it is a summer morning in the forest, that Robin carries or wears a horn and a bow, and that later the set will need to include or suggest the tree trunk. Ask the children to tell you any dialogue that can be transferred or adapted.

5. Before beginning shared writing, decide on three scenes that will be included in the play, for example: the first scene could be Robin leaving his Merry Men to go off in search of adventure, the second could be the confrontation with Little John, and the third could be Little John being welcomed to join the Outlaws.

6. Using the ideas from the beginning of the extract, write the first scene as a piece of shared writing (see the photocopiable sheet).

Independent work

● Give the children the photocopiable sheet opposite and ask them to plan the second and third scenes with a partner, using the outlines decided upon in the lesson, and to include useful production notes. Ask them to write up their work independently.

Plenary

● Compare and contrast the settings, events and characters in the second and third scenes that the children have just written.

Further support
● Some children may find it easier to write production notes after first quickly sketching some of their ideas.

A playscript

■ Make production notes on adapting 'How Little John Came to the Greenwood'. Scene one has been done for you.

Notes for SCENE ONE: Sherwood Forest, morning (*set to include green trees; sound effects could include birdsong; lighting to indicate summer morning*). Robin pacing around, restless (*Robin has his horn, bow and quiver of arrows*). Will and other Outlaws sitting or lying about (*one or two to be propped against tree trunks*). Robin and Will discuss lack of adventures; Robin leaves to look for 'sport'.

Scene	Where scene is set	Characters involved and brief description of what happens
Scene two		
Scene three		

Scenery/props: scenery needed for each scene and list of props for the whole production	Costumes: list of characters with costumes needed for each one
Lighting: when stage lighting on full, dimmed to give atmosphere, spotlights to be used and when, and so on	**Music/sound effects:** type of music used and when it is to be played, sound effects (for example, *storm, clock chiming, dogs barking*)

Recounting an event

Objectives

Y5. T1. T21.

To identify the features of recounted texts such as sports reports, diaries, police reports.

Y5. T1. T24.

To write recounts based on subject, topic or personal experiences for (a) a close friend and (b) an unknown reader.

Guided work

1. Ask the children what is meant by 'recounting an event'. Revise that it is a retelling of an event that has really happened. Display this list of features on the board or on a poster and discuss the points.

- Orientation/opening paragraph: introduces the subject – briefly sets the scene.
- Body of text: events recounted chronologically in sequence.
- Contains descriptive detail.
- Narrator's feelings and thoughts are included.
- Concluding paragraph summarises the main ideas.
- There may be an evaluation of the event.
- Language features: often a personal account, told in the first person (*I, me, my, we*) but can also be written in the third person (*he, she, they*); connectives help show sequence of events; powerful language used in description; mainly uses past tense.

2. Read photocopiable page 122 with the children. Ask them to work in pairs or small groups to identify features from the list displayed by annotating the text.

3. Discuss their decisions as a whole group, including details like:

- no opening paragraph – extract from the middle of a recount.
- chronological order – relating the final moments before the Titanic sank.
- powerful descriptive detail.
- narrator's feelings and thoughts written in the first person and past tense.

Independent work

- Give the children a copy of the photocopiable sheet opposite and ask them to plan and write the first draft of a recount of a recent event. Give them a topic to write about. Let the children tell their recount orally to a partner to help them practise the detail. Remind them to use the first person (*I, me, my, we*).

Further support

- To help the writing process, brainstorm relevant words and phrases with the children before they begin their plans. Display a list of time connectives for the children to use.

Plenary

- Choose a subject all the children have experienced, making sure it is not something that was written about in the activity. Ask the children to take turns to say a sentence recounting part of the day, trying to keep it in chronological order. You may want to start the game with something like: *The first thing I did this morning was....* Challenge the children to start with a time connective each time.

Recounting an event

Title:	Notes
Orientation/opening paragraph: (*introduces subject – sets the scene*)	
Main body of text: (*chronological sequence, descriptive detail, gives narrators feelings and thoughts*)	
Concluding paragraph: (*summarises main ideas, may evaluate the event – personal point of view*)	

Features to remember
- A personal recount is told in the first person.
- Events are sequenced in a chronological order.
- Language and connectives help to show the sequence of events (*for example, first, later, at the end of the day*).
- Powerful language should be used in description (*adjectives, adverbs and verbs*).
- Past tense is used.
- The author's feelings and thoughts should be included.

50 LITERACY HOURS FOR LESS ABLE
LEARNERS: Ages 9–11

Clear instructions

Objectives
Y5. T1. T22.
To read and evaluate a range of instructional texts in terms of their: purposes; organisation and layout; clarity and usefulness.

Y5 T1 T25
To write instructional texts, and test them out, for example, instructions for loading computers, design briefs for technology, rules for games.

Guided work

1. Ask the children to recall things that need instructions. Their suggestions might include directions to places, playing a game, a recipe, using a computer, design briefs in technology and so on.

2. Display photocopiable page 123, read the instructions with the children and establish what they will help the reader to do (store numbers in the telephone's memory). Remind them about the importance of sequencing in instructions and the use of imperative verbs (for example, *press, tap, enter*). Ask the children why we need the instructions and why the sequencing is important. Discuss the detail involved in the instructions and why point 6 is more detailed.

3. Remind the children that we need instructions for many different things. Write the following instructions on the board. Ask the children to work in pairs to make and play the following game.

> **1.** Make a set of 12 cards with a picture of a fruit on each one.
> **2.** Shuffle the cards and put them face down on the table.
> **3.** The first player turns over two of the cards. If they match, the player keeps them, if they do not, they are put back on the table.
> **4.** The next player takes a turn as above.
> **5.** The winner is the person who has the most matching pairs at the end of the game.

4. Ask the children for their comments about the instructions. Were they in sequence? Did they give enough information to make the game? Did they give enough detail to play the game? How easy were these instructions to follow? How could they be improved?

Independent work

● Give the children the photocopiable sheet opposite and encourage them to write their own instructions for making and then playing the game of 'Pairs' introduced in the lesson. Encourage the children to work together and to read through what they have written to check they have included all the steps and that they are in the right order. Let them play the game again, following their instructions.

Plenary

● Ask the children to swap partners and exchange their sets of instructions. Can they understand the instructions? Are they clear? Do they think they could carry out the process described? Then brainstorm what other activities a set of instructions is useful for around the home or at school.

Further support
● Make a list of words that could be useful in instructions, for example: *turn right, turn left, go straight, shake the dice, move forward, load, click, construct, measure, first, then, next.* Read the list with the children, add any others they suggest and display the list for them to use while they are writing.

Clear instructions

◼ Use this writing frame to help you write a set of clear instructions.

Materials and equipment needed: (for example, board or pieces for game, disk for computer, materials for technology)	

Title: How to...

Sequence of instructions: (what to do first, second, third and so on. Remember to use imperative verbs. Think about whether including a diagram would be helpful)

1.

2.

3.

4.

5.

6.

7.

8.

Abbreviations

Objectives

Y5. T1. T23.
To discuss the purpose of note-taking and how this influences the nature of notes made.

Y5. T1. T27.
To use simple abbreviations in note-taking.

Guided work

1. Revise work on note-taking from Years 3 and 4. Discuss the importance of making clear, concise notes by reminding the children about the purpose and requirements of note-taking.

2. Show the children the following sentence and ask them what they think it says: *Hse lvd in stb.* Can they work out what it is meant to say? (*The horse lived in a stable.*) Explain that when we take notes we often abbreviate words and use symbols. We need to remember how we abbreviate words or it could mean when we come to read them, they do not make sense or we misunderstand them. If, for example, the original sentence had been: *Hse in fld,* this could mean: *The horse was in a field* or *The house was in a field* or *flood!*

3. Display the following common abbreviations and symbols, then add any suggestions that the children have. Point out, if they do not suggest them, contracted words, such as *don't, you're* and so on.

4. Ask the children to work in pairs or small groups to invent abbreviations for common words or terms.

5. Dictate a few sentences for the children to jot down quickly, so they understand that notes do not need to be written down word for word.

PTO - please turn over	**‹** - smaller/less than	**Rd** - road
& - and	**›** - bigger/more than	**Mt** - mount/mountain
→ - to/go	**eg** - for example	**w/e** - weekend
Jan - January	**etc** - and so on	**vg** - very good
PO - post office	**NB** - note/danger/beware (from Latin nota bene)	**1st** - first
∴ - therefore	**St** - street	**ie** - that is
		Dr - doctor

6. Discuss the ideas that the children have come up with and how one person's abbreviations can be different from another's.

Independent work

● Ask the children to read each sentence on the photocopiable sheet opposite carefully and to work out what the abbreviations mean. Then ask them to write the sentence out with no abbreviations.

Plenary

● Ask the children to think of an abbreviation. Ask the first volunteer to write it on the whiteboard and the others to work out what it is. The child who guesses correctly writes their abbreviation on the board and so the game continues.

Further support

● Display the list of abbreviations from the lesson.
● Give guidance on reducing words (for example, by taking out the vowels as in *hse*).
● Help the children to identify key words to reduce a sentence to the bare bones, for example: The black dog was standing right in the middle of the road may be reduced to: Blk dog mid of rd. Compare it to text(txt)ing on mobile phones!

Abbreviations

◀ Rewrite these abbreviated sentences in full.

1. Chdn ➡ fly their kite in pk.

2. She ➡ London for w/e.

3. Jake lvs on Gordon Rd.

4. Whole fam walked ➡ Mt Snowdon.

5. Use map find cities, eg London, B'ham & Leeds.

6. Plse put book betw lamp & vase.

7. Liam vg in sch today.

8. Roof v low ∴ must mind head!

9. Kate > Hattie, but < Jo.

10. Mum & Dad ➡ Nottm on Sat.

11. Wouldn't get off plane – enjoyed so much.

12. Need ➡ learn new vocab for spell tst.

13. NB ➡̸ beyond point.

14. Imp top on tight so acid doesn't spill!

15. Volc was about to erupt ∴ peop must ➡.

16. ➡ PO turn 1st R., 1st L. & 2nd L. again.

Taking notes

Objectives

Y5. T1. T26.
To make notes for different purposes.

Y5. T1. T27.
To use simple abbreviations in note taking.

Y5. T2. T17.
To locate information confidently and efficiently through skimming to gain overall sense of text and scanning to locate specific information.

Guided work

1. Remind the children about the work covered in 'Abbreviations' on page 92. Do they remember why we abbreviate words when making notes? (So that we can write the notes quickly.) Remind them that it is important to understand any abbreviations made.

2. Ask the children why we write notes. Their suggestions might include leaving a message for someone, noting down times for buses or trains, making lists of things to do, instructions on how to get somewhere, taking down information from a book. Point out to the children that we take notes on the information given in books to try to obtain the facts most relevant to our interests or needs. Remind them that when we are researching a subject, we should always use two or three books to get balanced information, writing some notes from them all, and then put the notes into a logical order before we write our own information.

3. Display the first section of the photocopiable sheet opposite and ask the children to skim the text to get an idea of what it is about. Tell them that before we start to take notes it is important to make sure that the text is what we are looking for. It is then possible to find any key words and phrases by scanning to locate specific information, for example: significant dates and names and descriptions of trophies.

4. Work with the group making brief notes from the text.

Independent work

● Ask the children to make their own notes from the second text on the photocopiable sheet. Remind them to record the title of the work and author before beginning their notes, and use abbreviations which they will be able to read and understand when they come to use the notes again in the activity 'Non-chronological reports' on page 96.

Plenary

● Write a sentence in note form on the whiteboard and ask for a volunteer to make it into a full sentence, for example: *He* ➔ *pk to fd dcks.* (*He went to the park to feed the ducks.*) The children could also take turns in writing a full sentence for another child to abbreviate into a note, as short as possible but still understandable.

Further support

● Some adult help may be needed either with reading the texts or in picking out what to include in their notes. Help the children to spot and underline key words and remind them about using abbreviations.

Taking notes

◼ On a separate sheet, make notes from these two pieces of text, so that you can use them to write a report about the Olympics.

The History of the Modern Olympic Games

In 1894 a Frenchman, Baron Pierre de Coubertin, thought of resurrecting the Olympic Games, and so the first of the modern games was held in 1896. Twelve countries took part and it was opened by the King of Greece, in Athens, in front of a huge crowd.

The Los Angeles Olympics in 1981

The first medal of these very first modern games was won by James Connolly, an American, in the triple jump, with a jump of 13.71 metres. (Compare this to Jonathan Edwards' record of 18.29 metres jumped in 1995.)

The medals at this time were silver and only given to the winner of each event, but in 1908, when the games were held in London, medals were awarded to the first three places in all the events. Then in the 1912 games, held in Stockholm, electrical timing equipment was used for the first time in the running events.

The Ancient Olympics

The Ancient Olympic Games started in 776BC in Athens, Greece. They began as a religious festival and were held every four years. This tradition continued for a thousand years in a place called Olympia, just outside the city of Athens.

The Term of Pan, Olympic Stadium, Athens

The athletes trained in Olympia for ten months before each of the games, where they had to be examined by ten members of an Olympic panel. These assessors investigated the athlete's parents, physical strength and character.

From 776 to 724BC the only event was the foot race, *stade*, which was running the length of the stadium. The winner of this race in those very first games of 776BC was recorded as Coroebus of Elis. At later Olympiads, the 400 yards and then the 3.3 miles, or 24 *stadia*, were added events and by 680BC chariot racing had been introduced.

Non-chronological reports

Objectives

Y5. T2. T22.
To plan, compose, edit and refine short non-chronological reports and explanatory texts.

Y6. T1. T13.
To secure understanding of the features of non-chronological reports.

Y6. T1. T17.
To write non-chronological reports linked to other subjects.

Guided work

1. Tell the children that they are going to be writing a report and remind them about previous work on non-chronological reports.

2. Display a copy of the sheet opposite, to remind the children of some of the features that may be included in a non-chronological report. Read through the poster together and discuss the main points.

3. Give each child a copy of photocopiable page 124. Ask children to work in pairs or small groups and to identify which features of a non-chronological report are in the text.

4. Discuss their suggestions as a whole group. Try to ensure the following points are covered in your discussion.

> ● The short introductory paragraph states only vaguely what the report is about, without giving a definition or mentioning the main subject of the report (the World Cup).
> ● The main body of the text outlines the history and development of the World Cup competition.
> ● Each paragraph has a main idea and supporting details.
> ● It is factual, giving dates, statistics and information about significant teams.
> ● It is historical, so most of it is written in the past tense. It changes to use the present tense in the fourth paragraph when it reports about the tournament today.
> ● It does not have a summarising conclusion, but concludes with information about the World Cup for women's football.

Further support

● Ask the children to draw three or four boxes and label each with a main idea (for example, the first medal winners and the opening ceremony and so on). Then ask them to identify which notes should go as supporting details into these boxes. This will enable the children to organise their ideas before they begin writing. Remind them that it is more important that their paragraphs should be organised logically by topic, rather than chronologically.

5. Remind the children that when we are researching a subject, we should always use two or three texts in order to get a variety of details and different points of view, choosing appropriate notes to write from all the sources. Then these notes should be put into a logical order before we write our own version of the information.

Independent work

● Using the notes made as a group and individually on the two texts in the lesson 'Taking notes' on page 94, ask the children to write a non-chronological report about the Olympic Games. Give them a copy of the poster as a checklist to help them structure their reports.

Plenary

● Ask volunteers to share the way they organised their main idea and supporting details, asking them to describe why they chose to use those particular headings.

Non-chronological reports

The following are features that could help to identify a non-chronological report.

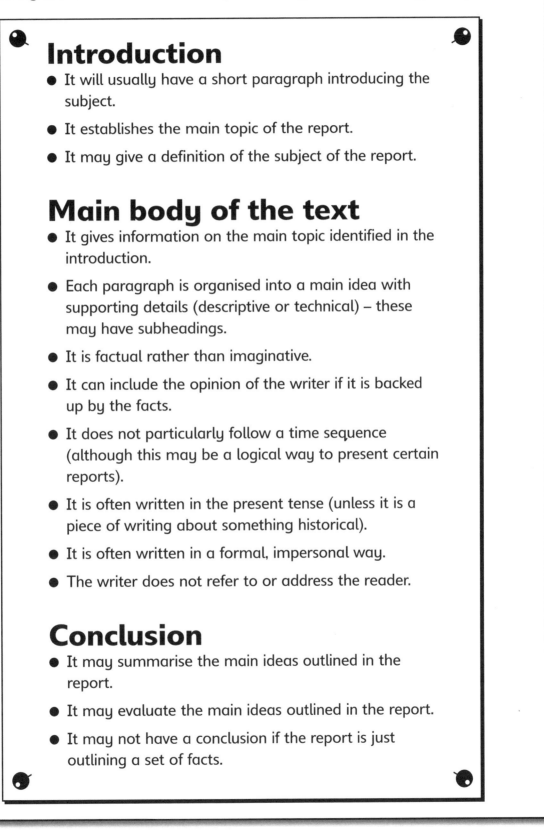

Introduction
- It will usually have a short paragraph introducing the subject.
- It establishes the main topic of the report.
- It may give a definition of the subject of the report.

Main body of the text
- It gives information on the main topic identified in the introduction.
- Each paragraph is organised into a main idea with supporting details (descriptive or technical) – these may have subheadings.
- It is factual rather than imaginative.
- It can include the opinion of the writer if it is backed up by the facts.
- It does not particularly follow a time sequence (although this may be a logical way to present certain reports).
- It is often written in the present tense (unless it is a piece of writing about something historical).
- It is often written in a formal, impersonal way.
- The writer does not refer to or address the reader.

Conclusion
- It may summarise the main ideas outlined in the report.
- It may evaluate the main ideas outlined in the report.
- It may not have a conclusion if the report is just outlining a set of facts.

50 LITERACY HOURS FOR LESS ABLE
LEARNERS: Ages 9-11

Persuasive writing

Objective
Y5. T3. T19.
To construct an argument in note form or full text to persuade others of a point of view.

Guided work

1. Remind the children about previous work on persuasive writing.

2. Display photocopiable page 125 and read it to the children. Discuss the following list of features typical of persuasive writing.

> *A persuasive text aims to win over a reader to a particular point of view.*
>
> **The opening paragraph:**
> - grabs the reader's attention
> - states the side of the argument the writing will support
> - puts forward some of the questions that will be form part of the argument
> - finishes by explaining the purpose of the writing.
>
> **The main body of text:**
> - each paragraph has a main idea supporting the argument, with examples and evidence to back up the case
> - arguments are general, but the author's views are presented
> - uses forceful, emotive language typical of argument
> - may include cause and effect
> - language is used which is appropriate to the reader
> - is written in the present tense or conditional.
>
> **The concluding paragraph:**
> - gives a summary with a restatement of the main argument
> - may give an appeal directly to the reader.

3. Ask the children to work in pairs to see which of the features in the list they can identify in photocopiable page 125, then discuss the text as a whole group.

Further support
- Display a list of useful words and phrases that the children may include as part of an argument.
- Some children will find it easier if they can discuss their ideas with a partner or in small groups before starting to make their own notes.

Independent work

- Ask the children to use the photocopiable sheet opposite to organise their ideas for a piece of persuasive writing. Ask them to plan a piece of writing to their parents or carers about why they should be allowed to join a new sports or youth club. Why do they want to join? What will it add to their lives? How it would help them?

Plenary

- Ask volunteers to outline their main arguments for wanting to join a new club. Then ask for a show of hands to see if the other children believe that parents or carers would be persuaded.

Persuasive writing

Theme of argument:

Notes for opening paragraph: (to grab attention, state the argument, outline the questions, restate purpose for writing. Consider to whom you are writing and why)

First argument: (main idea with supporting examples and evidence to back up the case, include cause and effect language, for example: *because of, then, as a result of, it is probable that, consequently* and so on)

Second argument:

Conclusion: (summary with a punchy, emotive restatement of main argument, appeal directly to the reader)

50 LITERACY HOURS FOR LESS ABLE LEARNERS: Ages 9-11

Biography/Autobiography

Guided work

1. Ask the children if they have read any biographies and, if so, who they were about.

2. Read photocopiable page 126 with the children. Help them to identify it as an extract from an autobiography. Remind them that an autobiography is the life story of a person written by him or herself.

3. Outline the features of an autobiography with the children including the points below.

- An autobiography aims to be a true recount of the writer's life so far (or part of it).
- It is told in the first person and it is assumed that the reader already knows a little about the writer (*my mother said to me; that was all I knew*).
- It is generally written in a chronological order, from birth, through childhood, to adult life, including references to dates or the writer's age (*When I was twelve; in September 1929*).
- There is more emphasis on presenting events plainly, rather than on atmospheric descriptions (*We were put on the train*).
- Each new phase of life is treated separately.
- It is mainly written in the past tense, although the ending may be in the present as the writer tells of his/her recent life.

4. Note those features that can be identified in the text displayed, as in the examples above, or ask the children to do this in pairs.

5. Go through the same process with the biography on photocopiable page 127. Note some of the main similarities and the differences between it and autobiography including the following points.

- An introduction to a biography often states why the subject is special or gives some basic facts.
- It is told in the third person.
- A conclusion usually evaluates the person's life and contribution to the world.

Independent work

- Give the children a copy of the photocopiable sheet opposite. Ask them to read each sentence and decide whether it has been taken from an autobiography or a biography.

Plenary

- Ask a child to say a line of a biography of someone else (classmate or famous figure) and see if the others know who is being described.

Biographies

◼ Read these sentences and decide whether they are taken from a biography or an autobiography.

1. Churchill was one of the greatest leaders the world has ever seen.

_____

2. After spending my first few years at Rowsley Infants, I then moved to Howarth Junior School.

_____

3. His first job was with the local newspaper in Crompton, his local town, as a junior reporter.

_____

4. On the morning of my wedding I woke up to the devastating news that the King was dead.

_____

5. Bannister's contribution to the world of athletics is still considered to be one of the greatest sporting achievements ever.

_____

6. Marie Curie won the Nobel Prize for physics in 1903.

_____

7. I went to war in February 1915, just after my 17th birthday.

_____

8. From her humble beginnings as a grocer's daughter, Margaret Thatcher became Prime Minister of Britain.

_____

9. After a while the job became easier as all of us 'new recruits' soon learned the ropes.

_____

10. It is almost impossible to know what to include and what to omit when writing about Henry VIII.

_____

11. He died on 6 February 1952, leaving his daughter Elizabeth to become Queen of England.

_____

12. I am told that I began talking very early, and by the time I was two years old I could hold a decent conversation.

_____

Writing a biography

Objective
Y6 T1 T14
To develop the skills of biographical and autobiographical writing in role, adopting distinctive voices, for example, of historical characters.

Guided work

1. Re-read photocopiable pages 126 and 127 with the children. Recall what types of text they are (autobiography and biography).

2. Revise the typical features of biographical writing examined in the previous lesson 'Biographies' on page 100.

3. Give the children a copy of the photocopiable sheet opposite and together, read through the notes about Scott of the Antarctic. Ask the children to work in pairs to cut out the strips and sort the information into a logical order. Then ask them to stick them on to another sheet to form a set of notes about Scott. Alternatively, the activity could be used on an interactive whiteboard. Suggest the following headings to help the children to organise the sentences.

> - *Introductory paragraph:* state the name of the person and why he is special. Perhaps give a basic idea of when he was alive or when his most important achievements took place.
> - *Main body of text:* in a chronological order; birth and childhood; experience of work; marriage and family life.
> - *Concluding paragraph:* evaluate the subject's life and contribution to the world.

4. Discuss how to expand the notes into a comprehensive biography the notes. Perhaps give an example of how the first set of notes could be developed into an autobiography in the voice of Scott, for example: *I was born on 6 June 1868 at a place called Outlands, near Devonport, in Devon and named Robert Falcon Scott. My mother, Hannah, and father, John, had five children in total, three girls and one other boy.*

Independent work

- Ask the children to use the rearranged sentence strips and notes they have just developed to write a biography of the famous explorer.
- Alternatively, you could ask them to write it as an autobiography, in the role of Scott. Help them to consider how to present the information from Scott's point of view. What will they have to leave out? (Information about his death and why he is remembered.)

Plenary

- Ask for three volunteers – one to read out the beginning, one the middle and one the end of their biographies. Do the biographies still make sense as the writer changes? If there is time, do the same with the autobiographies.

Further support
- Display the features of both autobiographies and biographies for use as the children work (see page 100).
- Ask the children to keep stopping and reading their work through to ensure consistency with the voice of the narrator and the verb tenses used, and that everything is in a logical, chronological order. Point out the dates as one way of helping with this.

Writing a biography

■ Cut out these strips and sort them into a logical order in preparation for writing a comprehensive biography or autobiography of Scott.

Robert Falcon Scott

British arctic explorer

Sailed in the ship – *Discovery*

Had one son – Sir Peter Markham Scott

Second expedition (1910–1912) 'Terra Nova' expedition reached South Pole 18 Jan 1912 but found Roald Amundsen got there one month earlier

Blizzards on return journey – all died – 29 March 1912 – 11 miles from safety at food and fuel depot

Married to Kathleen Bruce

Born 6 June 1868 at Outlands, near Devonport, Devon

Scott's and other bodies found eight months later

First went to sea aged 13 (1893) – as Midshipman on *HMS Boadicea*

Scott's diaries – published 1913 *Scott's Last Expedition*

Died 1912 on second exploration

Had three sisters and one brother

Mother and father – Hannah and John Scott

Carried on serving in Royal Navy until 1901

Remembered for bravery in attempting race to S Pole

First expedition to South Pole (1901–04) – failure – got to within 450 miles of S Pole – but had to turn back

A balanced report

Objectives

Y6. T2. T16.
To identify the features of balanced written arguments.

Y6. T2. T19.
To write a balanced report of a controversial issue.

Guided work

1. Read the article on photocopiable page 128 with the children. Ask them where they might find a piece of writing like this. Why do they think it is a cutting from a newspaper? What is it about?

2. Remind the children about any previous work they have done on newspaper reports.

3. Tell the children that sometimes journalistic articles only give one point of view, for example: if England were playing France at football, the match report in the British papers would probably be very different from the ones in the French newspapers the next day.

4. Discuss the following features with the children.

> ● *Headline:* punchy - short and snappy - eye-catching, often uses alliteration, for example: Becks Bounces Back.
> ● *Opening paragraph:* needs to hold the reader's attention, says what the report is about.
> ● *Main body of the text:* each new paragraph introduces a main idea with supporting detail, contains facts and eye-witness accounts to support argument; in a balanced report the different sides of the argument will be summarised - strengths and weaknesses given; mainly written in general terms but personal opinion indicated; uses third person and mostly past tense.
> ● *Conclusion:* summarises report; may evaluate subject or argument (make judgements on both points of view).

5. Ask the children to work in pairs or small groups to identify these features in the text on photocopiable page 128, then discuss their suggestions as a whole group.

Independent work

● Read the photocopiable sheet opposite with the children. Ask them to discuss in pairs both sides of the argument. Why have Mr and Mrs Peace brought in the local council and newspaper? Why would this make Mr and Mrs Barker angry? How could a journalist report this situation? Then ask the children, individually, to record some notes on the writing frame, which they will use later to write a balanced newspaper article (see 'News articles' on page 106).

Plenary

● Put the headings *The Barker family* and *The Peace family* on the board and ask the children to suggest reasons for and against keeping Tiny the dog. List their suggestions in the appropriate column.

Further support

● Display the list of features of news reports to help the children as they work.
● Some children may need help with words and phrases for expressing both sides of an argument, for example: *on the other hand, alternatively, conversely, however, contrary, the opposite point of view is, consider the other side* and so on.

A balanced report

There is a local dispute between two neighbours. Mr and Mrs Barker have a very fierce German Shepherd dog, Tiny, which barks loudly and frequently. Their neighbours, Mr and Mrs Peace, are frightened of the dog escaping and are kept awake at night by the barking. Mr and Mrs Peace have brought in the local council and newspaper, the *Weekly Tripe*, to try to solve the problem.

■ You are the reporter for the *Weekly Tripe*. Plan your article.

Headline: punchy, short and snappy, attention-grabbing

Opening paragraph: brief, interesting summary of the subject

The Peace family **First argument:** including eye-witness accounts, third person strengths and weaknesses given, past tense	**The Barker family** **First argument:** including eye-witness accounts, third person strengths and weaknesses given, past tense
Second argument:	**Second argument:**

Third argument/council's views:

Conclusion: summarises report, evaluates subject

News articles

Objectives

Y6. T1. T15.
To develop a journalistic style.

Y6. T1. T16.
To use the styles and conventions of journalism to report on for example, real or imagined events.

Guided work

1. Remind the children about previous work on news reporting and newspaper articles.

2. Display photocopiable page 128 and read it with the children to remind them about the style of a newspaper article. Discuss the typical genre features that can be identified (see 'A balanced report' on page 104).

3. Give the children enlarged copies of the photocopiable sheet opposite and read the article together. Do they notice how one-sided it is? Remind them that, sometimes, journalistic articles only give one point of view. Better journalistic reports take a more balanced approach. How could this article be more balanced?

4. Ask the children to work in pairs or small groups to discuss what they would add to or change in this article to make it into a balanced report. Encourage them to highlight and annotate the sheet. If necessary, prompt them by asking the following questions.

- How would the local children feel about being blamed for the rubbish and damage?
- Do they think that it is the local children who are responsible for ruining the parks?
- How would the children feel about having to stay indoors?
- What quotes would they want to see included to give the point of view of the local children?
- What could the town council do to maintain the parks after the refurbishment and cleaning operation?

5. Discuss their suggestions as a whole group.

Independent work

- Using their notes made in the previous lesson, ask the children to write a balanced report for the *Weekly Tripe* about the situation between the feuding neighbours. If possible, ask the children to word-process the article so that they can use desktop publishing to 'publish' their report with the style and layout features typical of a newspaper article.

Plenary

- Give the children a few scenarios (for example, a minor road accident involving a van delivering glue, a visit to school from a famous pop star) and ask them to come up with inventive headlines, for example: *Sticky Mess, Pop Star Pops In.*

Further support
- List the features of a balanced news report (see page 104). Also, if possible, display a selection of appropriate-level newspaper or magazine articles.
- Suggest that the children keep stopping to read what they have written so that they remain aware of the style of a newspaper article, the voice of the reporter and the verb tense that they are using. Also remind them to consider the readership, taking care to use appropriate language.

News articles

🖝 Annotate this report to consider how you would make it more balanced.

CHILDREN – KEEP THEM IN!

Local children are being blamed for the terrible state of the parks around the pretty seaside town of Hatterton, Glintshire. The three parks, Grant Lane, Turnbury Close and Rawlings Street, have now been closed to the public.

Residents living close to the parks have complained to Hatterton Town Council about the amount of litter, causing rats and other vermin to move into the area.

'It's a disgrace,' said Mrs Moaner, of Number 2, Grant Lane. 'Children are running about in the park at all hours of the day – dropping rubbish everywhere.'

Council officials were also informed of the damage to the children's play areas in two of the three parks. 'Swings have been pulled from their chains, the slide has been covered in sticky paint and the roundabout has been jammed so that it doesn't go round,' said an irate Mr Whinger, of 56, Rawlings Street. 'Parents should keep their children in the house.'

Mr Penpusher, a council official, said, 'We are doing all we can to get the parks reopened. Work is due to start this week on the repairs and clean up operations, and we hope to allow the public access again from the middle of June.'

Local residents have said that they will be keeping a close eye on the refurbishment of all three parks. 'We just need reassurance it won't happen again,' concluded Mrs Moaner.

50 LITERACY HOURS FOR LESS ABLE LEARNERS: Ages 9–11

Book reviews

Charlie and the Chocolate Factory
by Roald Dahl

For the first time in a decade, Willy Wonka, the eccentric chocolate maker, is opening his factory to the public - well, just a select number of the public. The lucky five who find a Golden Ticket in their Wonka chocolate bars will be invited to a private tour of the production line, given by Mr. Wonka himself. For Charlie Bucket, this is a dream come true. When he finds a 50-pence piece in the street, he can't resist buying two Wonka's Whipple-Scrumptious Fudgemallow Delights – even though his poor family could certainly use the extra money for food. But as Charlie unwraps the second bar, he sees the glint of gold under the wrapper! The very next day, Charlie, along with the motley crew of fellow winners Mike Teavee, Veruca Salt, Violet Beauregarde, and Augustus Gloop, steps through the factory gates to discover the truth about the Chocolate Factory and its mysterious owner. What they find is that the gossip is mild in comparison to the extraordinary truth, and for Charlie, life will never be the same again. *Charlie and the Chocolate Factory*, another unforgettable yarn from the legendary Roald Dahl, never fails to excite, delight, and captivate audiences of all ages.

Tom's Midnight Garden *by Philippa Pearce*

Tom's Midnight Garden by Philippa Pearce is one of my all time favourite books. The story centres on an amazing clock, which leads to a secret place with new discoveries. It is not an easy read, so some children may find they lack the imagination and understanding necessary to enter the other world in this unforgettably brilliant story. We first discover that the clock standing on the landing of Tom's aunt and uncle's house, has intrigued him from the moment he first saw it. In fact, it's the only thing of any interest that he can find in that old house! Tom is told firmly that it belongs to Mrs. Bartholomew, the owner of the house, and that he must never, ever touch it. Then one night, Tom hears it striking, and as he counts, he realises that it strikes thirteen. Intrigued, he comes downstairs to find a mysterious and wonderful garden that seems to magically appear only at that time. Inside the garden, Tom finds Hattie, a girl from another time, with whom he develops a close friendship. He soon discovers that time in the 'midnight garden' moves differently than the time in Tom's "real" world – it moves backwards and forwards and at a totally different pace. Within that garden, with Hattie, Tom learns about himself, about time, and how to reach across time. Philippa Pearce's time manipulation is created extremely cleverly; it is beautifully and intriguingly done, the clock being a significant symbol throughout the story.

HOW LITTLE JOHN
CAME TO THE
GREENWOOD

It was late in their first summer in Sherwood, and on a sudden Robin grew restless.

'Stay you all here, my merry fellows,' he said early one morning. 'But come and come swiftly if you hear the blast on my horn that you all know as my special call. We have had no sport these fourteen days and more: no adventure has befallen us – so I will go forth and seek for one. But if I should find myself in difficulties, with no escape, then will I blow my horn.'

Then he bade farewell to Scarlet and the rest, and set off blithely through the greenwood, his bow ready in his hand, his eyes and ears alert for anything of danger or of interest.

About noon he came along a forest path to a wide, swiftly flowing stream which was crossed by a narrow bridge made of a single tree-trunk flattened on the top. As he approached it, he saw a tall yeoman hastening towards him beyond the stream.

'We cannot both cross at once, the bridge is too narrow,' thought Robin, and he quickened his pace meaning to be first over.

But the tall yeoman quickened his pace also, with the result that they each set foot on the opposite ends of the bridge at the same moment.

'Out of my way, little man!' shouted the stranger, who was a good foot taller than Robin. 'That is, unless you want a ducking in the stream!'

'Not so fast, not so fast, tall fellow,' answered Robin. 'Go you back until I have passed – or may be I will do the ducking!'

'Why then,' cried the stranger, waving his staff, 'I'll break your head first, and tip you into the water afterwards!'

'We'll see about that,' said Robin, and taking an arrow well feathered from the wing of a goose, he fitted it to the string.

Roger Lancelyn Green

Kensuke's Kingdom

I tried to sit up to look about me, but I could not move. I tried to turn my neck. I couldn't. I could move nothing except my eyes. I could feel though. My skin, my whole body throbbed with searing pain, as if I had been scalded all over. I tried to call out, but could barely manage a whisper. Then I remembered the jellyfish. I remembered it all.

The old man was bending over me, his hand soothing my forehead. 'You better now,' he said. 'My name Kensuke. You better now.' I wanted to ask after Stella. She answered for herself by sticking her cold nose into my ear.

I do not know for how many days I lay there, drifting in and out of sleep, only that whenever I woke Kensuke was always there sitting beside me. He rarely spoke and I could not speak, but the silence between us said more than any words. My erstwhile enemy, my captor, had become my saviour. He would lift me to pour fruit juice or warm soup down my throat. He would sponge me down with cooling water, and when the pain was so bad that I cried out, he would hold me and sing me softly back to sleep. It was strange. When he sang to me it was like an echo from the past, of my father's voice perhaps – I don't know. Slowly the pain left me. Tenderly he nursed me back to life. The day my fingers first moved was the very first time I ever saw him smile.

When at last I was able to turn my neck I would watch him as he came and went, as he busied himself about the cave. Stella would often come and lie beside me, her eyes following him too.

Every day now I was able to see more of where I was. In comparison with my cave down by the beach, this place was vast. Apart from the roof of vaulted rock above, you would scarcely have known it was a cave. There was nothing rudimentary about it at all. It looked more like an open plan house than a cave – kitchen, sitting-room, studio, bedroom, all in one space.

Michael Morpurgo

The Phoenix and the Carpet

The bird rose in its nest of fire, stretched its wings, and flew out into the room. It flew round and round, and round again, and where it passed the air was warm. Then it perched on the fender. The children looked at each other. Then Cyril put out a hand towards the bird. It put its head on one side and looked up at him, as you may have seen a parrot do when it is just going to speak, so that the children were hardly astonished at all when it said,

'Be careful; I am not nearly cool yet.'

They were not astonished, but they were very, very much interested.

They looked at the bird, and it was certainly worth looking at. Its feathers were like gold. It was about as large as a bantam, only its beak was not at all bantam-shaped.

'I believe I know what it is,' said Robert. 'I've seen a picture –'

He hurried away. A hasty dash and scramble among the papers on father's study table yielded, as the sum-books say, 'the desired result'. But when he came back into the room holding out a paper, and crying, 'I say, look here,' the others all said 'Hush!' and he hushed obediently and instantly, for the bird was speaking.

'Which of you,' it was saying 'put the egg into the fire?'

'He did,' said three voices, and three fingers pointed at Robert.

E Nesbit

The Ghost of Thomas Kempe

It was the day of the centenary. The school was festive, and full of visitors all day. The people of Ledsham flowed in to look at the exhibition, see the school, and talk to the children. James, like the rest of the older ones, had a job to do showing visitors round and telling them about the work that they were doing at the moment. He spent a long time trying to explain a maths problem to an old lady who had difficulty with decimals and thought it was wonderful what children did nowadays, and an equally long time with Mr Dalton from the pub who turned out to be very interested in ancient Greece. But all the while, in one part of his mind, he was distracted. There was something required of him, but he did not know what it was. There was something he had to do, but he did not know how to do it. He stared at the portrait of Arnold, asking for help, but there was only Mr Arnold Luckett there, looking benevolent, with his gold watch-chain pulled tight across his stomach.

It was while he was on his own, looking at the old brown photographs and wondering which, if any, of the solemn little girls in white pinnies was Mrs Verity, that he felt Thomas Kempe. The sorcerer broke nothing, and slammed no doors, but James could feel him nonetheless. There was a constriction, a tightening of the air, but it was only for him: all around, people moved and talked unconcernedly. Mr Hollings hurried to and fro: a baby cried: someone called across the hall to a friend. 'What do you want?' said James, inside his head, and Thomas Kempe made a wall of air, as insistent as a wave at sea, and pushed James away from the table and into the classroom and then towards his own desk.

'What do I do?' said James, silently, and the lid of the desk rattled. He opened it, and the message was written on a piece of blotting-paper that lay on top of the exercise books.

> Helpe me to goe. Finde my resting-place, & putt there my pype & my spectacles.

'Yes,' said James. 'Yes. I will. But you'll have to tell me where.'

Penelope Lively

Time Trap

When I started this book, almost the first words I wrote were about circular insanity, do you remember? Well, let's get back to that thought and I'll show you just how circularly insane we've got.

The story so far: long ago, before I was born, Uncle Lipton went on the spaceshot to the Galaxy. He took the keep-young drug Xtend so that he would arrive at the Galaxy still a young man. If there hadn't been a Galaxy spaceshot, the scientists might never have invented Xtend. If they hadn't invented Xtend, Uncle Lipton would be dead and buried long ago and I would never have known him.

All right so far? Hold tight and we'll go further.

Because of Uncle Lipton, I was able to travel back through time. Because I travelled back through time, I was there when Axel Stern baled out with his parachute. Because I stopped Axel Stern bleeding to death, he lived.

And then what happened? Axel Stern, German pilot, became Axel Stern, spacecraft inventor and pioneer. It was Axel Stern, more than any other man, who got Uncle Lipton into space, heading for the Galaxy.

Now you can see where the circular insanity is coming in. But I'll spell it out for you anyway...

I wasn't even born when Axel Stern should have bled to death after his dogfight. Yet I saved Axel Stern from bleeding to death

Uncle Lipton went on the Galaxy spaceshot only because a man who should have been dead was saved by a boy who hadn't yet been born.

Xtend was invented to preserve life during spaceshots; however, Xtend might never have been invented if Axel Stern hadn't lived. But then, if Xtend hadn't been invented, I wouldn't have been able to travel back through time. And if I hadn't been able to travel back, Axel Stern would have died and there might have been no need for anyone to invent Xtend.

I like that last paragraph, I really do. The more you read it, the less sense it makes.

And that's what I mean by circular insanity.

Nicholas Fisk

50 LITERACY HOURS FOR LESS ABLE LEARNERS: Ages 9-11

THE SECRET GARDEN

She slept a long time, and when she awakened Mrs. Medlock had bought a lunch-basket at one of the stations, and they had some chicken and cold beef and bread-and-butter and some hot tea. The rain seemed to be streaming down more heavily than ever, and everybody in the station wore wet and glistening waterproofs. The guard lighted the lamps in the carriage, and Mrs. Medlock cheered up very much over her tea and chicken and beef. She ate a great deal, and afterwards fell asleep herself, and Mary sat and stared at her and watched her fine bonnet slip on one side until she herself fell asleep once more in the corner of the carriage, lulled by the splashing of the rain against the windows. It was quite dark when she awakened again. The train had stopped at a station and Mrs. Medlock was shaking her.

"You have had a sleep!" she said. "It's time to open your eyes! We're at Thwaite Station, and we've got a long drive before us."

Mary stood up and tried to keep her eyes open while Mrs. Medlock collected her parcels. The little girl did not offer to help her, because in India native servants always picked up or carried things, and it seemed quite proper that other people should wait on one.

The station was a small one, and nobody but themselves seemed to be getting out of the train. The station-master spoke to Mrs. Medlock in a rough, good-natured way, pronouncing his words in a queer broad fashion which Mary found out afterwards was Yorkshire.

"I see tha's got back," he said. An' tha's browt th' young 'un with thee."

"Aye, that's her," answered Mrs. Medlock, speaking with a Yorkshire accent herself and jerking her head over her shoulder towards Mary. How's thy missus?"

"Well enow. Th' carriage is waitin' outside for thee."

Frances Hodgson Burnett

Blurbs and synopses

Blurb for *The Thieves of Ostia* by Caroline Lawrence

The year is 79 AD.
The place is Ostia, the port of Rome.

Flavia Gemina, a Roman sea captain's daughter, is about to embark on a thrilling adventure.

The theft of her father's signet ring leads her to three extraordinary people – Jonathan the Jewish boy next door, Nubia the African slave-girl, and Lupus, the mute beggar boy – who become her friends. Their investigations take them to the harbour, the forum, and the tombs of the dead, as they try to discover who is killing the dogs of Ostia, and why.

The first of the Roman Mysteries is an exciting whodunnit that tells you just what it was like to live in Ancient Rome.

Blurb for *The Hodgeheg* by Dick King-Smith

Max is a hedgehog who lives with his family in a nice little home, but unfortunately on the wrong side of the road from the Park. The beautiful Park with its Lily-Pond, and more importantly its slugs, worms and snails just waiting to be gobbled up by hungry hedgehogs!

The busy road is a dangerous barrier but Max notices that humans seem to cross it quite easily. If they can, why can't hedgehogs? So begins his courageous, hair-raising quest to lead hedgehog-kind to greener pastures. His first attempt ends in a nasty bump on the head, and Max finds when he tries to speak his words are all mixed up. He is now a hodgeheg, not a hedgehog, but nothing will distract him from his misson.

Synopsis of *The Hodgeheg* by Dick King-Smith

Max is a hedgehog who lives with his family on the wrong side of a busy road from the Park, where there is an abundance of slugs, worms and snails. Max, seeing that humans are able to cross quite easily, decides he will find a safe way for hedgehogs to cross too, but with his first attempt he gets a bump on the head. This leaves Max all mixed up – and he becomes a hodgeheg!

At his second attempt he gets another bang on the head, which restores his speech back to normal, but Max is still determined to find that safe hedgehog crossing.

He eventually succeeds when he follows some 'small humans' who cross with a 'great big female' – and the whole hedgehog family can now cross the road safely with the school lollipop lady!

50 LITERACY HOURS FOR LESS ABLE LEARNERS: Ages 9-11

School poems

First Day Back

First day back at school
Children clean and neat
New coats hang on coatpegs
New shoes shine on feet.

School hall smells of polish
Toilets smell of soap
Children meet new teachers
Faces full of hope.

Teachers give new books out
Children start new page
Up the curtain rises
On the same old stage.

Allan Ahlberg

The Question

The child stands facing the teacher
(This happens every day);
A small, embarrassed creature
Who can't think what to say.
He gazes up at the ceiling,
He stares down at the floor,
With a hot and flustered feeling
And a question he can't ignore.

He stands there like the stump of a tree
With a forest of arms around.
'It's easy, Sir!' 'Ask me!' 'Ask me!'
The answer, it seems, is found.

The child sits down with a lump in his throat
(This happens everywhere),
And brushes his eyes with the sleeve of his
coat
And huddles in his chair.

Allan Ahlberg

Animal poems

Cat's Funeral

Bury her deep, down deep,
Safe in the earth's cold keep,
Bury her deep –

No more to watch bird stir;
No more to clean dark fur;
No more to glisten as silk;
No more to revel in milk;
No more to purr.

Bury her deep, down deep;
She is beyond warm sleep.
She will not walk in the night;
She will not wake to the light.
Bury her deep.

EV Rieu

The Hippopotamus's Birthday

He has opened all his parcels
    but the largest and the last;
His hopes are at their highest
    and his heart is beating fast.
O happy Hippopotamus,
    what lovely gift is here?
He cuts the string. The world stands still.
    A pair of boots appear!

O little Hipppotamus,
    the sorrows of the small!
He dropped two tears to mingle
    with the flowing Senegal;
And the 'Thank you' that he uttered
    was the saddest ever heard
In the Senegambian jungle
    from the mouth of beast or bird.

EV Rieu

50 LITERACY HOURS FOR LESS ABLE
LEARNERS: Ages 9-11

Write-A-Rap Rap

Hey, everybody, let's write a rap.
First there's a rhythm you'll need to clap.
Keep that rhythm and stay in time,
'cause a rap needs rhythm and a good strong rhyme.

The rhyme keeps coming in the very same place
so don't fall behind and try not to race.
The rhythm keeps the rap on a regular beat
and the rhyme helps to wrap your rap up neat.

'But what'll we write?' I hear you shout.
There ain't no rules for what a rap's about.
You can rap about a robber, you can rap about a king,
you can rap about a chewed up piece of string …
(well, you can rap about almost … anything!)

You can rap about the ceiling, you can rap about the floor,
you can rap about the window, write a rap on the door.
You can rap about things that are mean or pleasant,
you can rap about wrapping up a Christmas present.

You can rap about a mystery hidden in a box,
you can rap about a pair of smelly old socks.
You can rap about something that's over and gone,
you can rap about something going on and on and on and on …

But when you think there just ain't nothing left to say …
you can wrap it all up and put it away.
It's a rap. It's a rap. It's a rap rap rap rap RAP!

Tony Mitton

SCHOLASTIC

Maggie and the Dinosaur

Maggie ran madly round the museum –
And what do you think she saw?
A mighty tiger whose grin grew wider,
Fishes and fossils galore:
And stretching up to the ceiling
Was a rattling dinosaur.

'I'm only made of wire and bones,'
The dinosaur seemed to say;
'Everyone stands and looks at me,
But nobody wants to play.'

Maggie just froze in amazement,
Watching the dinosaur's jaw:
He spoke in a dusty whisper,
Not an earth-shattering roar.

She tried to pretend this was normal
As they passed the time of day,
Waiting until the attendant
Was looking the other way.

The dinosaur groaned as he shifted his bones
All the way to the lift,
But when the door slid open
Maggie knew he just wouldn't fit.

And so they made a break for it,
But Maggie took great care
That nobody would notice them
As they shuffled towards the stairs.

Every time they met someone
The dinosaur stopped on the spot,
And people said, 'Look – another one!
We thought we'd seen the lot!!'

They slithered slowly inch by inch
Across the entrance hall,
Then the dinosaur doubled his neck up
To squeeze through the double front door.

He clattered down the steps outside,
Running into the sun
Towards a brightly painted van
That attracted everyone.

When Maggie managed to reach him,
The dinosaur was near to tears:
'This is what I've waited for
For two hundred million years!'

A look of unspeakable happiness
Spread across his face –
But as people stared at the dinosaur,
He just gazed into space.

'I've tasted nothing like it,
It's a marvellous magical dream,
It's all I ever wanted –
A freshly whipped strawberry ice cream!'

Dave Ward

Humorous verse

Ettykett

My mother knew a lot about manners,
    she said you should never slurp;
you should hold your saucer firmly,
    and not clang your teeth on the curp.

My father knew nothing of manners,
    all he could do was slurp;
and when I can't find a rhyming word,
    I set about making them urp.

John Rice

Where Teachers Keep Their Pets

Mrs Cox has a fox
nesting in her curly locks.

Mr Spratt's tabby cat
sleeps beneath his bobble hat.

Miss Cahoots has various newts
swimming in her zip-up boots.

Mr Spry has Fred his fly
eating food stains from his tie.

Mrs Groat shows off her stoat
round the collar of her coat.

Mr Spare's got grizzly bears
hiding in his spacious flares.

And ...

Mrs Vickers has a stick insect called 'Stickers'
and she keeps it in her ....

Paul Cookson

I Saw a Jolly Hunter

I saw a jolly hunter
    With a jolly gun
Walking in the country
    In the jolly sun.

In the jolly meadow
    Sat a jolly hare
Saw the jolly hunter.
    Took jolly care.

Hunter jolly eager –
    Sight of jolly prey.
Forgot gun pointing
    Wrong jolly way.

Jolly hunter jolly head
    Over heels gone.
Jolly old safety-catch
    Not jolly on.

Bang went the jolly gun
    Hunter jolly dead.
Jolly hare got clean away,
    Jolly good, I said.

Charles Causley

Haikus

Four Seasons Haiku

I.

yellow rapefields glow;
hedges dipped in mayblossom:
cream in a green bowl.

2.

flags hang limp from masts;
buddleias flop exhausted
on August pavements.

3.

folding up fruit-nets;
already a trawl of leaves
in their green meshes.

4.

take away one word:
a tall chimney collapses
in the winter wood.

Adrian Henri

Haiku

Snowman in a field
listening to the raindrops
wishing him farewell.

Roger McGough

Haikus

Swaying in the breeze,
Their heads nodding, bluebells ring,
Heralding summer.

Grey as steel, the sea
Shimmers in the fading light:
Day slides into night.

John Foster

50 LITERACY HOURS FOR LESS ABLE
LEARNERS: Ages 9-11

My voyage on the Titanic

People wrestled with the oars and rowed desperately. Squeezed towards the bow of our lifeboat I plunged my right arm into the freezing water up to my elbow. My attempts to help paddle away from the sinking ship were useless. I gave up and held my numbed fingers inside my coat like a young Napoleon.

'Row for your life!' a grey haired man was yelling. 'Before we get sucked under!'

Panic stricken, those with oars clashed their shafts against each other and our boat began to drift back. The stricken ship's stern was levered into the air, two huge propellers pointing to the heavens. Even if the mighty engines that powered them could have been put into reverse it would have had no effect. A man who had jumped off the ship, to plummet metres into the sea, swam towards us and was hauled aboard. After his rescue, the old man took charge again.

'Pull… pull… pull,' he shouted. Our boat surged forward away from the din of shattering glass and creaking metal, which groaned under the immense strain. There was a vast explosion causing clouds of smoke to billow from the Titanic's front funnel before it ripped from the superstructure. The steaming column hit the water sending a mighty swell towards us, our exhausted oarsmen doing well to keep their rhythm as the boat pitched at a dangerous angle on the wave.

Though we had put some distance between the doomed ship and ourselves now, my heart sank for the people who clung to its deck. With horror I could hear their dreadful screams as the colossal hull steadily slid into the ocean. Even if the helpless passengers had jumped into the sea at the last minute and been able to find lifejackets, they had little chance of surviving. The abrupt extinguishing of all the ship's lights confirmed the end as it descended into a freezing darkness. With a stately grace the ship finally slipped beneath the waves.

The unsinkable had sunk.

Eugene Blackwood

☼ Memory dialling

Your **HAPPIFONE 2005** has **50** memories for storing telephone numbers of up to 20 digits.
The name of each phone number can be stored using a maximum of 8 characters.

To store a number in memory:

1. Press the **LIST** button

2. The digital display shows **FONEBK**

3. Press the **YES** button

4. The digital display shows **ENTER**

5. Press the **YES** button

6. The digital display shows **NAME?**
   The buttons **2** to **9** give the letters, depending on how many times you press e.g.:

   > **1** is a space,-,1
   > > **2** is A, B, C, 2
   > > > **3** is D, E, F, 3 ... etc.

7. Tap in the name

8. Press the **YES** button

9. The digital display shows **NUMBER?**

10. Enter the number using the buttons, using the **CS** button for any spaces

11. Press the **YES** button

12. The digital display shows **ENTER** again. You can continue to store more numbers in your **HAPPIFONE** or press the **LIST** button to go back to the standby mode. 🐾

The World Cup

Before 1930, there was no international tournament for professional footballers. The most important competition was in the Olympic Games, but this was for amateurs.

FIFA (the organisation in charge of international football) made plans to stage a professional tournament and chose Uruguay as the host country. Uruguay had won two Olympic football golds and was celebrating its centenary in 1930. In July 1930 the first football World Cup was staged.

13 teams took part from around the globe: 7 from South America, 4 from Europe, and Mexico and the USA. No British teams were involved, as they were not members of FIFA at the time. The winners of that first World Cup were the hosts, Uruguay.

Since then, the World Cup has been held every four years, although none took place in the 1940s because of World War II. The tournament has become one of the most important and popular sporting events in the world and is watched by huge numbers of football fans of all ages.

The number of teams taking part has also increased over the years. In 2002 there were 36. There are also more countries wanting to take part, so there are qualifying rounds before each tournament.

So far, only seven countries have ever won the World Cup. Brazil have taken part in every tournament and have won it five times, including 2002. After their third win, in 1970, they were allowed to keep the original trophy. This gold trophy had been named after the FIFA president who had founded the tournament in 1930, Jules Rimet. The current trophy, the FIFA World Cup, has been passed on to each winning team since 1974, although each winner does get to keep a life-size replica.

Since 1991 there has also been a World Cup for women's football. The first was held in China for 12 teams and was won by the USA. In 2003 16 teams entered. The winners were Germany.

Persuasive text

The Editor
The Grimwold Chronicle
Upper Street
Grimwold

Dear Editor

Well done to Grimwold Council for deciding to build a skateboard park! We skateboarders have been waiting a long time for this, but at last we can celebrate!
However, I should like to make it clear to the people of Grimwold that we will certainly not abuse the great opportunity that we have been given.

I know that a lot of older people in the town think we don't deserve this park. I think they must forget that they, too, were young once! Surely they must realise that it is not so easy to have fun these days without getting into trouble. There is nothing much else to do in this town. For example, we get told off by the parents of smaller children if we hang out with our mates in the recreation ground, and we get chased off by the cops if we use our skateboards in the streets or on the car park. Surely, it is better that we have an area of our own, where we can enjoy ourselves well away from adults. It is clear that the new skateboard park will benefit everybody – not just us skateboarders!

It seems obvious to me that we are bound to look after this park when it is built. After all, we would be the ones to suffer if it got smashed up. I can tell you that if any non-skateboarders try wrecking it, they will have us to reckon with! If the skateboard park has a proper wall around it to help keep down the noise, I can assure people that we will do our best not to upset them. After waiting all this time for our own skateboard park, we will be not be giving anyone the chance to throw us off it!

So, come on you people of Grimwold, give us a chance to prove that we deserve this park. You won't regret it!

Yours faithfully

Fred Finnegan

Fred Finnegan (11)
Publicity Officer
AFS (Action For Skateboarders)

Getting dressed for the big school

When I was twelve, my mother said to me, 'I've entered you for Marlborough and Repton. Which would you like to go to?

Both were famous Public Schools, but that was all I knew about them. 'Repton,' I said. 'I'll go to Repton.' It was an easier word to say than Marlborough.

'Very well,' my mother said. 'You shall go to Repton.'

We were living in Kent then, in a place called Bexley. Repton was up in the Midlands, near Derby, and some 140 miles away to the north. That was of no consequence. There were plenty of trains. Nobody was taken to school by car in those days. We were put on the train.

I was exactly thirteen in September 1929 when the time came for me to go to Repton. On the day of my departure, I had first of all to get dressed for the part. I had been to London with my mother the week before to buy the school clothes, and I remember how shocked I was when I saw the outfit I was expected to wear.

'I can't possibly go about in those!' I cried. 'Nobody wears things like that!'

'Are you sure you haven't made a mistake?' my mother said to the shop assistant.

'If he's going to Repton, madam, he must wear these clothes,' the assistant said firmly.

And now this amazing fancy-dress was all laid out on my bed waiting to be put on. 'Put it on,' my mother said. 'Hurry up or you'll miss the train.'

'I'll look like a complete idiot,' I said. My mother went out of the room and left me to it. With immense reluctance, I dressed myself.

First there was a white shirt with a detachable white collar. This collar was unlike any other collar I had seen. It was as stiff as a piece of Perspex. At the front, the stiff points of the collar were bent over to make a pair of wings, and the whole thing was so tall that the points of the wings, as I discovered later, rubbed against the underneath of my chin. It was known as a butterfly collar.

Roald Dahl

THE LADY OF THE LAMP

Florence Nightingale (1820-1910) came from a wealthy, English family. She was much admired in London for her nursing work. Sidney Herbert, the Secretary of State for War, asked Florence to gather a team of nurses and set sail for the Crimea.

When she arrived in Turkey, Florence was appalled by the conditions in Scutari Barrack Hospital. She worked 20-hour shifts, converting the filthy, rat-infested wards into a cleaner, brighter, more efficient hospital. Florence's work at the hospital reduced the patient death rate from 42 per cent to just over 2 per cent.

Her patients adored her. They called her "the lady of the lamp" because of her habit of roaming the wards at night with a lantern, checking on their comfort and welfare.

By the time Florence returned to England, she was a national heroine. She went on to write about the importance of diet and sanitation for good health. She also began raising money, which she used to found a nursing college, the Nightingale Training School for Nurses, in London.

In 1907, Florence Nightingale became the first woman to be awarded the Order of Merit, which is given to British citizens in recognition of a great contribution to society.

Richard Dungworth

Image © Ingram Publishing

Newspaper article

Grimwold Chronicle

GRIMWOLD'S SKATEBOARDERS JUMP FOR JOY

A decision last night by Grimwold Council to provide a skateboard park in the town has delighted local youngsters. But older residents are concerned about the cost, and have expressed fears about noise and vandalism. Dozens of young people from the pressure group AFS (Action For Skateboarders) demonstrated outside Grimwold Town Hall as councillors met to discuss the controversial plans. When they heard that the decision had gone their way, the demonstrators celebrated by putting on an impromptu skateboarding display in the market place.

Shoppers interviewed today by the *Grimwold Chronicle* were split in their views. "I think it's disgusting," declared Albert Grump (82). "When I was a boy, we had to make our own pleasures, like playing cricket with a piece of wood and a ball made up from two pairs of socks. I don't see why I should pay my council taxes to spoil the kids with this kind of nonsense."

"I worry about the noise that this is going to create," said another shopper, Lily Gentle (50). "There are elderly people's flats close. In any case, the park is bound to be vandalised as soon as it is built."

Other townspeople supported the scheme. Mother-of-two Felicity Fitchett said she was all in favour of giving young people in the town somewhere to go to let off steam.

The Council's decision to go ahead with the park is sure to create a lot more passionate debate before the skateboard park is built. The Mayor, Cllr George Solomon, assured the Chronicle that every effort would be made to locate the park in a position where it would cause as little nuisance as possible.

"I want to emphasise that this Council is determined to meet the needs of young people of Grimwold. They have been asking for this facility; we will trust them to look after it as well as enjoy it."

The final word must go to young Peter Pratt, an 11-year-old skateboarding enthusiast who spoke to the *Chronicle* when we found him practising his jumps on the wall around the car park. "This news is magic," he declared. "It'd be really cool if Grimwold produced a gold medal winner when skateboarding is finally accepted into the Olympics!"